Grief

The Guide to be Unguided

by Anneliese McDaid

Copyright © 2021 by Anneliese McDaid

All rights reserved. No part of this book may be reproduced or used in any manner without written permission of the copyright owner except for the use of quotations in a book review. For more information, address: grieftheguidetobeunguided@gmail.com

FIRST EDITION

Grief

*Dedicated to you, Mum,
forever in our hearts and minds!*

Love, your wee gorgeous x

Preface

This book follows the process of losing my mother during a world pandemic. It will cover a variety of forms of grief as my life tends to be quite the tale to tell, or so I am told. I wanted to get my thoughts and feelings down while they are raw and still at the forefront so that in grief, there is a sense of normality for you, or at least that is my hope. Guilt tends to eat us up when people die, and I think that is totally wrong! Guilt should not consume anyone. Feeling guilty because someone has died when it wasn't in any way your fault, is wrong, and we do that to ourselves the majority of the time. Why, though? There is no need for it. Let it go.

In this book, I will go over my feelings toward my Mum dying, and to some, it will seem shocking because they have never felt grief. And that is ok because one day you will feel it. It will all make some sort of sense to you. Now I want to say this loud and clear; everyone should be and will be telling you this when you are grieving, but there is no right or wrong way to grieve! Everyone's experience is different, but in my experience, being open about exactly what we feel is definitively crucial to our survival. Holding in a single thought or feeling is never a good idea at all. In fact, it is a truly awful idea, to be honest with you.

To go through all of my grief will require a brief history at some point, so it might take me a while of fumbling in the dark to find my way to the point, but bear with me. I do not think you will regret it. This book details some of the most horrible things I have endured. It is not for the faint-hearted. It will not be an easy read for most. Certainly not for anyone who knew me or my Mum, and had no idea this was all happening to us.

If I can help touch or influence a soul with this, I will be so happy to have helped anyone. Hopefully, it gives you a sense that your feelings during times of tragedy and horror are normal, and that pretty much all of us have or will feel it at some point. Even though in the moment you think that *no one* else on this earth could possibly know what it is like to be you, to be in your head and know how you are feeling. Well, I am here to hopefully clear that up for you, or at least let you know you are *not* alone! We are all out here living the best way we know how, having followed in the footsteps of our parents. At your loneliest moment, at least one million - give or take, will feel the exact way you feel. With nearly eight billion people on this planet, you can rest assured that someone knows what you are going through!

So, without further ado, here it is - I hope that my personal statement about my life, thoughts, and feelings help you along your journey on this incredibly astounding place we call Planet Earth.

I must confess that I am no writer at all, but I hope I can make this work well enough to inform and inspire at least someone.

Contents

Preface — vii

CHAPTER 1
Where to begin… — 1

CHAPTER 2
Lockdown Hit! — 9

CHAPTER 3
A Glimpse — 27

CHAPTER 4
Stephen Dying — 33

CHAPTER 5
Losing My Best Friend — 45

CHAPTER 6
Back in Time — 53

CHAPTER 7
Being Mum and Dad — 63

CHAPTER 8
The Abuse (My Biggest Grief)   85

CHAPTER 9
The Light   101

CHAPTER 10
Court   109

CHAPTER 11
The Hang Man   125

CHAPTER 12
Mum's First, Second, Third Attempts   135

CHAPTER 13
Out in the cold   145

CHAPTER 14
Gran   153

CHAPTER 15
Jacquie   159

CHAPTER 16
The Silence   171

CHAPTER 17
The Dreaded Day!   177

CHAPTER 18
The Weight   195

CHAPTER 19
Grief   215

Acknowledgements   247

About me   251

Chapter 1

Where to begin...

I lost my Mum during the 2020 global pandemic that was the coronavirus, COVID-19.

If truth be told, it was a terribly awful time, and I will start this story at the beginning of that year, going into greater detail about my life as we go on. So, I apologise now if I jump back and forth, veer off on five different conversations, and then finally come back to the point at hand.

2020 began with a blow for me right away.

In January of 2020, I was at work one day with my colleagues – I run a kitchen – and my Mum phoned. She would not have called if it was not important, so I stepped out and took her call. She asked me if I had heard about my Dad. She and Dad were not together and had not been for years. I replied, no, why? She went on to say that she had received a call from my auntie that my Dad had gone missing!

The previous year I got married to my best friend in the world, Matthew (or Matt). My Dad had elected to stop talking to me around Christmas of 2018 for many reasons that I will explain and expand upon later. So, I panicked, wondering why this could possibly have happened at all. Mum did not have much information at this moment, so I took it upon myself to message Dad's girlfriend, Denise, who replied immediately; Dad had been missing at least overnight is what I made of it She and Dad had been together about eight years at this point. He had found out he had cancer, and he decided to not face this news well at all. He left because he could no longer work at the time, and it was eating him up inside knowing Denise was the only one out earning a living. He left, and to this day, who knows where he really went. Maybe he went to a five-star hotel, or maybe he was really in a field like he claimed. We will never really know.

This was all very worrying for me and Dad's girlfriend, as Dad was not well at that time. He suffered from strokes and had open-heart surgery, so was required to take lots of meds. He had not taken a single one of the medicines with him. I thought to myself so many times during this period that I was going to lose my Dad at the age of twenty-nine. More times than I care to admit I thought, "This is it. I am going to lose my Dad.". He was missing for the entire weekend until we finally got in touch with him. He had sent a text to Denise and later followed up with a call. So, we knew he was ok at least, but we did not know where he was or why he had been there. He then said he might need an ambulance, and Denise was ready to do that right away if need be. He ended up not needing the ambulance. He made it home while Denise was at work and went for a long bath and a sleep. That weekend was truly like someone holding a gun to my head who was waiting a long time to pull the trigger, and then finally, they let you go. I had to call my Area Manager and Line Manager to keep them up to date and let them know that at any second, I might need to leave as my Dad might show up in a less than desirable condition.

My Mum was so excellent that weekend with me, willing to drop everything and come to me if I needed her. She had done it before when Dad had a bad stroke. So I knew she would do it this time.

She called for updates, wanting to know if Dad was ok even though she was very mad at him for not being at my wedding. She was able to put that behind her, and just be there for me. Which, to be honest, was a bit of a first. However, she was there, no matter what. I decided enough was enough, and that I had to go and see my Dad (he lives down south) as he could not avoid me then. Mum said I was brave to do such a thing, and she wished me the best of luck.

In March, the pandemic was getting quite serious, but we were all still very ignorant about it, and no one realised that we would end up in a lockdown as a result of it.

My husband Matthew and I went down south to see Dad from the first to the fourth of March on the Megabus, as it was the cheapest way to get there. It was a long and tiring trip, trying to get through London during a pandemic, with people seeming to not care at all, then having to go on the London underground (I almost had a full-scale panic attack in that situation). How we made it there and back and did not get the virus, I will never know. I am glad we did not catch it though. We headed to our accommodations which I had acquired quite inexpensively on booking.com. There, we dropped off our things and got ourselves together. I had sent my Dad's partner a photo of the station when we arrived to make her aware that we were there. At that point, I had not told them I was going at all. So, surprise!!

We decided to eat first before going to face the music. We chose a place called The Green Man, not far from our accommodation. I remember I could barely eat my pie at all. Matthew had no issues finishing his, while he quietly listened to me raving about the million outcomes of this visit that my anxiety had put into my head. We ate up, paid the bill, and booked an Uber to come and pick us up to go to Dad's. As we got there, I could see Dad out with the dog. I practically leaped out of the car, and because he was not expecting to see me, he had only glanced at me and did not realise it was me at first. I said "HELLO!" and he looked again.

"Oh, my god, what are you doing here?" he asked me, but all I could do at this point was hug him. I explained that I was there to see him, given all that had happened a few weekends prior. I had to wait to go because of money, but we managed in the end. I made Dad put the kettle on and make us all tea. We all acted like nothing had happened as if he had not missed our wedding and stopped talking to us. In these circumstances, you put these things behind you. You wait until a better time arises to speak of them, and him dealing with cancer was not the time to start being annoyed or angry about past events. It was just too inappropriate to do. So, we had our tea along with a few awkward moments when no one knew exactly what to say.

As the days went on, Dad started to open up and explain why he ran, and why he felt he had to do that. He revealed his feelings about his cancer, being shocked by it, and having a sense of tiredness he had never felt before in his life. I noticed it myself; he had lost a lot of weight, he was slower, he was not the same. His body simply could not cope with it all at that time. He had already survived so much with the strokes and his heart; his body was trying to slow him down for at least a moment. A few years prior he had a bad stroke, and if I remember correctly, he was back to work two weeks later! He most definitely should have taken a longer recuperation time before returning to the job. To be honest, it makes me question his employer at the time for allowing him to come back so quickly. I personally do not think I would have allowed my own staff to come back so quickly, even if they felt they wanted to; showing more consideration for the health, safety, and general well-being for them and for the other staff.

Dad was sick and that was evident. We had a good couple of days together and mended our bond because as I say, do not let the past be what grounds you. Let the future be what leads you out of the ground and lets you float around to see all there is to see out here in the world.

My husband and I got home from that trip, and I was fully convinced that my Dad was going to die; he had the big C and he was definitely going to be going into the ground very, very soon. I remember having a conversation with my former best friend (which we will go into later) about how I knew at some point in the younger years of my life I would lose a parent. But I did not think it would be at the young age of 29. I am acutely aware that 29 is not the youngest age to lose a parent, but as statistics go, actually it is pretty young. I remember explaining to him that I always felt with both of their health being, well…not really great, that I would lose my parents younger. I didn't think it would be in my 20s. I explained my cold feelings about it to him, and how at times I felt the cold acceptance that it was inevitable that they would die on me young. I also felt that given my Dad's health history, it would be him. It is worth pointing out here we were still waiting to find out how advanced Dad's stomach cancer was, as he had avoided going back to the doctor after he found out. He did finally go back, and we will go into that later. I remember thinking sad, depressing thoughts through it all. Was I going to be the second of the cousins on my Mum's side to lose a parent? Was this my destiny? My cousin lost his mum, my Mum's sister, and my aunt, in 2018. Her death was really a shocker, and more detail on that will follow; it is quite a story. Prepare yourself for that one.

I asked myself questions such as, "Did I expect it to be my Dad first?" or, "Did I think it would have been Mum?". Dad's health made me think it would be him, but then Mum's health was no picnic either, so who could really know.

The parade of thoughts and questions was endless. I remember wondering if we would need to pay to get his body moved from down south to Scotland. How much did that cost? Was he insured? Did that matter? All I thought about was funerals; Dad's partner and I discussed the financials of it for a bit just in case the results came back that he had stage four. All you do is panic, and I suffer from anxiety when it comes to matters like this; I like to over-analyse these situations to try and take myself through every possible outcome even before they arise. I think my Mum somehow bestowed that upon me. Not a bad trait to have, but not a good one either to be honest with you. It can be positive because you are rarely overwhelmed by information, as you have already thought it out and you are able to deal with a situation better in ways you can control, and your mind can process and deal with it better. I should point out I am not by nature a negative human as a result of this at all.

That was the start of the year. What a great start to 2020.

Chapter 2

Lockdown Hit!

Lockdown came around the second half of March, not long after we had returned from Dad's. I cannot remember the official date offhand. I do remember that the announcement of pub closures came first on a Friday evening. The announcement was an incredible feeling of awe and a vast sense of fear, sadness, and worry. We were told at 5 PM to close the doors, and that was it; we were done for a while. We did not know how we would be paid or anything. It was such a time of uncertainty for everyone. The whole world at once. It was insane. At the time of writing this, we are still in lockdown, awaiting a vaccine to be widely dispatched, hopefully very soon. As for the way we are all living, the permanent damage is not going to be clear to us for a long time now. Whatever psychologists write about this will definitely see them earn their PhD.

We are lucky enough to of had a furlough scheme in place in Scotland to provide some level of income during the lockdown. This small stipend allowed a little peace of mind. Unfortunately, my Mum and Dad were both evaluated and ranked at what was called extremely high risk, meaning they both had to go into complete self-isolation, even when the rest of us did not, as we were healthier with no underlying conditions. My Mum did not take this too kindly at all from the beginning. It took myself, Dad, and my Auntie Kellz - my mother's youngest sister, to call her and tell her she had to leave work, and that she could not be out and about in this madness. She did not really understand it or seem to care.

Let me side-track; Mum suffered deeply from depression. She had been on a variety of medications for a long, long time. For her, being trapped at home on her own was a fate worse than death. Mum and I lived quite far apart, which was made to seem even further away in a pandemic where neither of us could drive. Fourteen miles is a long way away.

She knew she would be cut off from the world and left in a house alone with her thoughts and feelings; a dread must have been in her like no other. Now, we were all there if and when she needed us, no problem. Calling and texting every day, or whenever she felt the need to see someone or talk to someone, we were there.

Before the beginning of the lockdown, my Mum had been seeing an idiot of a human being, John. We recognized that this was a massive mistake when he decided to come and try to take Mum out of her house and move her into his house. He wondered why we were all so mad at him. He kept telling me he loved my Mum and would not hurt her! Except, he could have killed her!

This pandemic was no picnic and had my Mum caught this virus she would have died all alone in the hospital. You see, Mum has COPD which is a serious lung condition formed from years of smoking. Yes, you may be thinking smoking is a choice, and she did that to herself, and you would be right, she did. My Mum had stopped smoking for over four years, which is amazing given she started the habit at eight years old. YES, eight years old! Absolute madness, but when my Mum was young, smoking was made cool through TV and such and they did not know how bad cigarettes really were. She had done so well to get off the cigarettes; it is a very difficult thing to do, especially for someone who suffers from mental illness, which I think can make it worse. I think your addiction centre is worse when you suffer from depression, and if you have a dependency it is a little harder to kick such a habit for good. People from Mum's work had given her cards to recognise being off them for a year, as this was HUGE for Mum. Anyway, back to the point.

She met this buffoon of a human being, who obviously has his own issues. To take someone with a serious health risk in a taxi to your home, while you have been frequenting the shop for your cans is not acceptable, especially when it is my Mum! Of course, I was outraged and lost my head! My Mum sensibly went back home, after Kellz and I had made her acutely aware of the risk she put herself in by allowing that to happen. However, I could understand it from her point of view; she just did not want to be on her own. Which is all well, fine, and fair enough, but not when you are putting your life at risk in such a way. I obviously did not want to be burying my Mum at my age of 29. So, anything I could do to prevent that, I would do it. She went back home in a huff, but that was fine. I could deal with any fallout that occurred afterward, as I have always done in my life. Mum's mental health was all over the place most of the time.

I segregated her in my mind and addressed her that way in person if she turned on me. She was Mum to me usually, but when she took a turn, she was Mary. Mary was the other side of my Mum that was mainly presented to me and me alone to see and deal with. She did allow others to see it at times, occasionally my auntie had dealt with a few of Mum's, for lack of better words, outbursts.

You see, Mum had a different way of being when she drank, which was once a week at least, and she would turn into a profoundly nasty, horrible person who would cut you to the bone. I had to segregate her in my mind for my own mental health and well-being. It was beneficial for Mum, as you could be a lot more assertive with her. Over the years, I had learned that that was the best possible strategy and helped her understand at those times that she had taken things a little too far. It worked to help make her see sense and rationalise her thought process. Occasionally this approach did not work, and she was still mad at you, no matter what you tried with her. Still, being assertive was my most successful way of getting through to her. Now, not everyone is the same and not everyone will react that way. If you can relate to any of this, though, you should give it a wee bash.

Remember, helping someone with severe mental health issues is not easy and it can be horrendously soul-destroying for them and you. It is absolutely ok to take a breath and remember to take care of your own mental health at these points as well, you know? You are important too. Often in my thirty years, I have had to take a step back from Mum to allow myself to realign my thoughts and energy. You cannot help someone if you are not of sound mind yourself, and more so if they are the cause of the disruption. Take some me-time every now and again!

So, back to the story of 2020. Mum fell out with me for making her come home, for being mad at her, for wanting to make sure she lived. When it comes to mental health and being a child to a parent with those difficulties, you often find that you are the adult to the parent most of the time because of the depression. My Mum was often childlike in nature, and a fight with her was extremely hard going. You were trying to reason with her, but there was no reasoning with her at all. Kellz and I had to give Mum an ultimatum about her 'friend'. It was us or him!

Let me explain why. Mum met this guy John not long before my wedding the previous year. We were married in August; Mum must have met him in June or July, but certainly, that is when she first mentioned this man to me. I had even offered to invite him to our wedding with her as a date, but she was not keen. It was too big an event for a date, she thought. They met on some kind of Facebook group for memes; and at the beginning, all seemed well and good. I was even eager about it. I was already wondering and imagining what it would be like at Christmas if Mum actually did bring someone with her, letting my imagination run away from me.

My Mum did not date; it was not her scene. This was quite a big thing for her. My Mum had been single for basically my whole life. She and my Dad split up when I was four years old, and she had never really been interested in being with anyone after that. I personally think that was a mistake on her part. She really deserved to find a nice man who would treat her right and want to get to know all sides of her. Unfortunately, it was not to be. Mum always said she did not want a man because she did not want to have to share her remote control with anyone; that was hers! They could not have it. I always found this wildly hilarious. She was definitely set in her ways. No man at all would be coming into her home and upsetting the balance she had put in place.

So, when she had mentioned John, I was of course a little shell-shocked. I asked loads about him, and she was a little stand-offish at first, which was to be expected. She was not yet sure about this relationship, so she did not want to divulge loads of things and have it amount to nothing. Mum was a private person most of the time; this is how they were raised. Old fashioned, and everything had to be kept a secret or "swept under the carpet," as they say. Not good at all for one's mental health. She decided to tell me a little more about this person as time went on. He seemed nice, and she had been over to his house, he had made her dinner, ran her a nice bath, etc. Then he added me on Facebook, and I had messaged him about my Mum back and forth. One night I messaged him because the Celtic and Rangers game was on; he, being a man of the blue team, and me, being a woman of the boys in green. Mum had told me he liked a good laugh and a joke about that sort of thing. He was messaging me about how my team were rubbish, and his were going to win. I then made a joke about how he would not be invited to Christmas dinner if there was any more of his crap, how I would cancel his and Mum's date that was coming up on Thursday. Of course, I was joking and having a laugh, as he had previously been. He turned on me extremely fast at this point and said something pretty mean, and he wasn't kidding about it either.

Mum had been with me all day that day as it was a Monday; that was her day with me. She had left to get her train, and she messaged me as she always did to tell me she was home safe, but also to say that John had cancelled their date on Thursday. I was shocked! I knew it had been my fault, but obviously not on purpose. Mum was ready to write him off there and then. I calmed her down and explained that he did not know me and maybe he just did not know I was kidding him. I advised her not to misjudge him and noted that she has done similar things in the past, so not to prejudge. Telling her to just give him a few days, and explain to him I was joking and see if he comes around. I also told her that if this ever happened again, then she should think about writing him off as once for Mum is enough. Mum needs stability, consistency, and positivity in her life, and if he was actually going to be this way all the time, we knew she didn't need that. So, she and I agreed everyone deserves a second chance, and if he did it again, that would be it.

Well, of course, he did it again, only worse this time. He let her down. I told Mum to get rid of him, and she said she would not be putting up with that again, not for a second time. Yet, somehow, she did. Somehow, he was still in her life and tormenting her.

My Mum had elected to tell this man her full life story, which was a huge deal for her. She did not really talk about the ins and outs of her life in depth to anyone at all. The fact she opened herself up to him meant that all the things I had been doing with her were working. Between the doctor and I, we had finally managed to get her thoughts to become clear and her mind in order. She was opening up to a relative stranger about things she normally wouldn't, because she previously lacked the confidence to do so.

Well, he decided to go on Facebook with this information and humiliate her. This had been such a huge step forward for my Mum, so for him to do that took literally years of progress off of my Mum's mental health. In fact, in my opinion, he basically undid all the good her psychiatrist and I had achieved over the last few years to get her in a position of confidence. We helped her feel confident about her ability to walk in her own skin and feel good about who she was, accepting her life story and recognising everything she had to be grateful for. He undid it ALL with that one stupid and petty action.

Now, I know I have stated previously that this man needed a lot of help himself. Did he know it? I think he did; I also think he saw my Mum coming from a mile off and thought that she was a target for a man of his demeanour. I think he preyed on her a little, knowing that in his eyes, she was weak. My Mum was a lot of things, but weak was not one of them. She did, however, suffer from a mental illness that caused poor reactions when it came to being vulnerable, which to be clear is not a weakness at all. With the life my Mum had, the fact she made it fifty-six years on this earth is astounding!

Her life was horrible and tragic, but she managed it. She was still here fighting the good fight and let me tell you when I say the word "fight" I truly mean that from her perspective. My Mum had a horrible childhood. I will be taking you into the story of my own childhood, and I want you to keep in mind that my Mum's childhood was truly and absolutely horrific. I am not going to go into the details of it; that was Mum's story to tell, and not mine to share in this book. When you see what she went through in my thirty years on this earth you will be thinking, my god that is awful. You will be right in thinking that my Mum had dealt with a lifetime of troubles before she was eighteen years old.

I have told so many people since she passed away, you know the saying 'you have made your bed so now you need to lie in it'? Well, I personally feel that someone else made my Mum's bed and she was fucked into it! Excuse my language, but it really does seem that way at times.

Back to this man. Other things had happened between them that she did not tell me at the time, as I imagine she knew I would not react well to them. He told her he loved her, and she was everything, beautiful and kind, etc. He then told her, "Here, I mean that hair will need to be changed, as it makes you look old!" or, "I mean these clothes will have to go, they are a state!". All these small statements would slowly but surely drown her in self-doubt, death by a thousand cuts. Self-doubt was something she had overcome with me. In October 2019, I had managed to get my Mum into the best mental state she had ever been in during my whole life. And then along came this man! This seedy, spineless man who tore down everything we had built by playing games with my Mum's head! His behaviour is that of a narcissist, which he clearly is.

He had continued to go to Mum's even after my aunt and I had given Mum the ultimatum, she still had him over. While I have no proof of this matter at all, I believe he regularly hit my Mum! I know he definitely had done it once, as she told us about it just after she had a full mental breakdown during lockdown, which we will go into more in a second. It was not actually until after my Mum died that I started to think about this, and obviously anger set in on me. I remember Mum and I had been sending photos of sunburn to each other, and in one of them, her eye was so swollen. I asked her what had happened and she said she had gotten something in it, and it was irritated. I believed her then, but now I am not sure that I do. Personally, I think it was him. A few photos later, she also had a massive bruise on her chest. Now, when my Mum was at work (she worked in Asda, a supermarket chain), she was always covered in cuts and bruises because she was like that, but being stuck at home, she could not really do much to cause that condition. So, I believe it was him. There is absolutely nothing I can do about it now. All I know is this man destroyed every ounce of my Mum's ability to think clearly; he destroyed any confidence that woman had built up in her own mind again.

So, as we get to April, my cousin Stephen who had been suffering from cancer for two years had taken a massive turn for the worst, and he unfortunately passed away on the 24th of April, which was only days before my Mum's birthday on the 28th of April. This was not good for Mum's mental health at all. I had to call and tell her as well; unable to go in person, which was just an awful thing to do. She was so upset by it, and on her own in her house. Not an ideal situation right in the middle of a full-scale lockdown. Stephen's younger sister, my cousin Jaime Marie, decided we would slightly break the lockdown rules for Mum's birthday on the 28th in light of the circumstances. We had all been in lockdown for over a month and not seen a single soul, so we knew we could not have contracted the coronavirus, but also took the proper precautions.

She came and picked my husband and I up from our house in Glasgow to go to Coatbridge to surprise my Mum.

My Mum was absolutely over the moon; she was so funny and thrilled to see people. Real live people, especially me. We did not even know if we would be able to go to my cousin's funeral at that point, as funeral gatherings were limited at the time due to the coronavirus outbreak. We were unsure about going as our family is quite big. We were, however, able to go; we got to say goodbye to him and be there to support the family.

I should mention that on the day of my cousin's funeral, I went back to Mum's afterward and had some lunch with her. As soon as we got home, her phone rang and she immediately and abruptly said, "Don't answer that!". I would not have any way, it's not like it would have been for me. The answering machine picked it up and guess who it was? Her male friend. The one who she had assured us she had no contact with, who she had blocked on all platforms and was out of her life completely. The same man that when my Mum had tried to get rid of him for good, left her so many voice messages on all devices that none of them could take any more messages at all; they were all full! He had sent her so, so, so many WhatsApps, Facebook messages, and texts too. He was a disease that just would not leave her alone! I was furious! I acted cool, though, as I knew she was struggling, and we had just been to her nephew Stephen's funeral, who was only thirty-five.

I stayed calm as she called this lowlife back and I could hear him saying to her so possessively, "I have been trying to get hold of you for ages, where have you been? You should have been back ages ago! I have called and messaged you so many times, Mary. I just wanted to know you were ok and nothing bad had happened to you!". We had been held up from what he would have deemed her time due back home because the family had arranged a lovely tribute to Stephen outside the funeral home, with a parade of muscle cars and so on, as Stephen was a car fanatic. After this, we then spoke to our family for a while, as you should do given everything that was going on. I then said to Mum, "Seeing as you have not been out in ages, how about we walk home?" It was a nice day after all, and I was with her so she was all good. We walked home together and she was chatting about how nice it was to be outside and to be with people again. Out on a nice walk rather than being stuck in the confines of her garden, she was just enjoying it all.

I could hear him asking her how the funeral had gone, and she was explaining how nice it had been, and how much he would have loved it. Stephen was a Rangers fan, and they had lots of Ranger's tops on as well as hanging out of car windows. He began to enquire about me, and took to shouting over the phone, "I love your mother, Anneliese. Can you hear me? I love her!". I could tell by Mum's face she was somehow enchanted by this cretin; after all he had done to her and everything he had put her through, she was still infatuated by him for some reason or another. I think there are many reasons for this. From my Mum's point of view, it had been so long since she had pictured herself with a man in her life, or had any man at all tell her she was pretty and kind and a great person, and that they wanted to be with her. I think due to her lack of self-esteem and confidence she fell for it all, I still maintain he had seen her coming and used her. To him she was prey with a target on her back, someone he could manipulate and control. As an example, my Mum did end up dyeing her hair for him; this was after they had actually stopped talking to each other, sort of! So, he impacted her thought process completely.

My Mum was unaware I was coming the day of her birthday, and I had told her to wait for me to call before she opened her presents. My Mum thought it was only going to be my aunt and cousin she would see.

GRIEF

When we all got there, Matthew and I hid around the back with her cake and a bottle of prosecco with plastic glasses. I could hear her say, "The wain hasn't even fucking phoned me yet to let me open my gifts, Kellz!". As she was saying this, I snuck up behind her and sprinkled confetti all over her! She screamed and started crying her eyes out, as she was so happy to see me and Matthew! She then began to open her presents, and she screamed the whole street down when she found out I had got her tickets to go and see Paul Weller! Her dream man and crush since she was a teenage girl. She even had her hair cut to match his at one point, which was a boy's haircut and not often seen on a young girl in those days. I remember her telling me she'd done it to annoy my grandad, which I found rather amusing.

I should also mention that we were all booked to go to Berlin in June for Matthew, my husband's 30th birthday; this was one of Mum's dreams, to go to Germany. At this point, we were still hopeful we would get to go. I had decided to pay to bring my Mum and let her live out one of her dreams. She taught me a small amount of German, and my name is also German, 'Anneliese', so I wanted to take her. She was so chuffed to have seen us and then she also got to see me on the day of the funeral, too. That was good for her. May was a rather quiet month really in terms of drama; if there was any. Mum certainly wasn't telling us about it. Our trip to Berlin was, of course, cancelled, but we rebooked it for November 26th; a nice early Christmas vacation. Germany in the winter was so beautiful anyway! A chance to visit the Christmas markets and surely this coronavirus thing will have blown over by then, or so we thought. Travel would be allowed by November, we hoped, which was also when her Paul Weller tickets were for. In June, Matthew's thirtieth came around. We had people come and see him outside the house that day for a few proseccos and a laugh. Mum was able to come along to that and be with us, which was a great little adventure for her.

She and I discussed that day about having my Dad up for Christmas dinner that year. You see, I always had my Mum for Christmas; she and I adore Christmas to the point of annoying those around us. She came every year on the 24th, and she made our soup starter for the next day and popped it in the fridge, then we would all go to the pub for a few beverages. We would come home at closing time, and all wake up on Christmas morning to me blaring Jive Bunny's Christmas remix, which my Mum had done when we were kids, as she had it on vinyl. She was so keen for Dad and his partner Denise to join us that year; we were all thrilled about it! When I did finally get back to work later that month and opened in July, I told every person I could that that year I would be able to spend Christmas with my mum and Dad, something I had not done since I was three years old. They split when I was four but Dad was gone before Christmas. My first ever memorable Christmas with my parents was coming, and I could not wait for it! It was going to be amazing.

Not long after Matthew's 30th, my Mum had a full mental breakdown. My aunt attended to her, as she lived not too far from my Mum. We could tell that something had been wrong with Mum that day, because we had not heard from her in a few days, and none of us could get a hold of her. When we finally did, she hit us with massive piles of abuse so Aunt Kellz took it upon herself to go down and see what she was up to. She had to call the police on my Mum, as she was being completely abusive toward her. Not a first for me really; I was used to her being that way. She was absolutely steaming drunk, screaming abuse as I was on the phone with my aunt while this was all happening. My Mum had been arguing with her to take back her phone and all her tablets, as that's all we wanted apparently. I was to take my phone back, she screamed at Kellz! I paid for my Mum's phone, as she could not afford to on her own. She was also very weird about online banking and paid everything in cash all the time. I wanted her to have a nice phone where she did not need to worry about topping it up and such, so I popped her onto my Tesco mobile account, which then made it a family account where you get great perks.

I can't imagine where this urgent need to try and give me this phone back came from. It seemed to have come recently during lockdown, where she had done the same thing when Kellz and I confronted her about this 'man' in her life, and she again said I should take this phone back, and give her the money. To make this clear, I saved money for my Mum. She would come to our house and give me cash to keep for her, to be used for birthdays, Christmas, or whatever she needed it for. This time she was saving for Berlin, so I had a lot of money put away for her. I always agreed and said I would give it back to her, as it was her money, not mine. Occasionally during arguments, she would grudgingly tell me to keep the money and spend it on something nice for me. She did not care, because no one cared for her. This was Mary we are talking about, no longer my Mum. She screamed at the top of her lungs at my aunt "ANNELIESE, FUCK OOOOOOOOOOOOOOOOOOOFFFFF FFFF!!" through the phone to me. The anger in her was unreal, but that was mainly the 1.5L of rum she drank over the course of 24 hours. I could tell she was literally shaking as she shouted it; it took all her might to project her voice in this way! The police arrived for her, and they made her leave with my aunt. That night they gave her three options, 1. Go with Kellz and stay the night there. 2. Kellz can stay with you. 3. We take you to a hospital, as we cannot leave you alone like this. It was clear to the police officers that she was a danger to herself and others.

She elected to go and stay with my aunt. There, she sat in a huff most of the night, muttering to herself. We knew she had been in contact with her 'man friend' for sure, and that he must have upset her a lot! The drinking had come out of nowhere! The next day I asked where Mum was, and they said they had taken her back to her house, so I got the train to go to her. I told her I was coming, she opened her door and looked at me like I had done something wrong. I went and sat in her living room, where I asked her what the chat with the man was? Why had she done this? At this point, she showed Matthew and I a bruise on her arm which her 'man friend' had kindly put on her. She said it was an accident, but even if it was, we had our doubts and it was unacceptable under any conditions. The story was that they had an argument and Mum had told him to get out and he refused. She grabbed the phone to call for help or the police, and he tried to grab the phone and punched her in the arm. Now, whether he meant to punch her or not is not even the worry. Why was my Mum so scared of this man that she felt the need to call for help?

I remember Mum telling me a few months after all this that he was telling her he would kill people in her family and asked, "Did she know how easy it was for him to get a gun?". He told her how easy it was for him to find out where people lived and worked, and so on.

This man had done prison time for armed robbery in his past. I am a firm believer in the fact people can change. Mum had mentioned this to me near the beginning of them seeing each other. I straight away said to her, do not write someone off because of their past. People can change and it is all dependant on his attitude toward it all now. Was he reformed? Did he know what he did was wrong, and that it should not have happened? Has he decided to use his past as a means to live a full and positive life now? I think at the beginning Mum thought he was good and that he had changed, or maybe thought she could fix him. To be honest, I do not really know. I can see how my Mum was so easily taken by him. She thought absolutely nothing of herself, and here came this man into her life telling her so many beautiful words and things about herself. Things she did not see, things she did not believe, things she did not know how to believe. She was taken in by the notion of someone liking her at all. I had her at the gym and eating better, and she was in a good headspace at the time, so it would have been easier for her to let this man in and take on a new challenge for herself. A hopefully successful venture was to be ahead of her. Unfortunately, she got a complete vulgar low-life of a human being instead of what she surely deserved, which was love and kindness and some understanding from this person.

As I mentioned earlier, I definitely believe this man had hit my Mum., There were photos that now started to make me think he had hit my Mum more than once! I also worry to think she suffered more from him as well. The day that I was there seeing her, and she had the bruise that she had sort of explained to us, we told her to take this whole matter to the police. She absolutely refused to do this saying, "Oh, no, I couldn't do that at all, you don't understand. He has told me things! I could not betray his trust like that. That is not me!". To which we retorted, "Simply, none of that matters, Mary! You need to go and get this guy dealt with. This is now physical and mental abuse.".

It was harassment; she asked him to leave her alone so many times and he would not. He was leaving so many messages on her phone that there was no room left for any more messages on any of the devices she had as well. He sent her so many messages. He played with her mind like a fiddle, giving her mountains of abuse in one sentence, then telling her he loved her and he still cared in the next. Now, Mum does that to me, or should I say did that to me, due to her depression. And maybe this 'man' has his own issues; well, I mean, clearly, he does, but he never cared to begin to help himself at all. That is not someone my Mum needs in her life. I also believe I have every right to be angry about this, this man's ability to destroy my Mum's happiness. She did not have much in her to begin with, and she and I worked really hard to build that back up and this, for lack of a better word, ARSEHOLE comes into her life and tears it all apart. Takes everything Mum and I took a long time to build and rips it to shreds! Yes, I am brutally angry at this human being! He really was warped and twisted, he needs to get serious help and to gain a sense of understanding or compassion for others! Empathy is in us all. I just do not understand how you can be that way without trying to help yourself. Why would you feel the innate need to drag another human being down with you? To drag a soul into your darkness. I understand we are ALL capable of accidentally hurting people we love in times of extreme pain and grief. I really do! Why would you drag a stranger into your life just to destroy their life? I cannot wrap my head around that at all.

Chapter 3

A Glimpse

After this, we managed to settle Mum down, make deals with her to stay away from this guy, keep him away for good, and start coming over to visit me every Monday as she was used to. She started coming to me on a Monday as she always did, and spent the full day with us. We took her out walking in the sunshine, as for living in Scotland, we actually had a really great summer thanks to global warming. A message would always be exchanged on the Sunday to confirm her time of arrival; she would base that on how I or she was feeling that day. Usually, it was the 10 AM train, meaning she got here at around 10:49 AM. Mum was a regimented soul, she liked order and punctuality, these were of the utmost importance to her. That is why Mondays were *our* days. I had to take a Monday off from my work no matter what, and if I did have to work, I had to give her so much notice and a good explanation as to why she couldn't come that day. She was understanding about it, but you had to make sure she was given plenty of notice of these events and changes.

I run a kitchen, so when big events or bank holidays fall on a Monday, I would need to work that Monday because it is a huge day of sales, as you can imagine. I was able to give her plenty of notice, so she did not feel any anxiety about it, or feel that I just did not want to see her. People who suffer from mental health issues need order and notice, otherwise life feels like chaos to them in these moments, and then they over analyse the whys of it all. I suffer from anxiety myself, so I can fully understand this. Mum would arrive expecting her tea to be ready to be poured upon her arrival. If not, I received a good slagging for it not being ready which was Mum's and my ways. If you have ever seen *The Gilmore Girls* and you were able to keep up, then you would have been able to keep up with Mum and I. We were both extremely quick-witted with each other, a good laugh most of the time. She would come in, have her tea, and ask what was for lunch. We would have lunch, go to the gym and meet my husband there, or on the way there from him finishing his day at work.

If the weather were to be particularly good, she would come nice and early and we would go to the gym earlier than usual, then go for a walk. A nice fifteen to thirty thousand steps to get that step count on the up, which is something I used to always go on about to my Mum, the importance of fitness and mental health. Vitamin D as well. Mum often gave me those set of eyes, as if to say here we go again, Anneliese going on about things that she knew were true and right; she just did not want to hear it anymore. I knew telling her over and over would help her take it in and really process the information. Lock it in her brain for good; it was working, too. Every week she came in and told me right away that she had been drinking plenty of water, getting her mini-home workouts done (this was before lockdown) that I had given her links to YouTube for. So, she was getting to grips with the right things that help us human beings to feel better. The body needs the right tools to function; without them, you are no good. Your body is a literal machine, and you can only get out what you put into it. So, if you put oil down a drain it eventually blocks the drain. Well, if you put shit into your body, you will only get shit back out of it. So be very aware that if you suffer from any sort of mental illness, start by fixing your small habits first, then you will notice all the other things you used to find overwhelming will begin to fix themselves.

On a sunny day, we would buy lunch on the move and take it to the botanical gardens in Glasgow, which is not too far from where I live. On occasion, we would take it down to the transport museum. This was a further walk, and we would sit there down by the Clyde and eat lunch in the sun. Often, we would video call my Dad and Denise to make them jealous, which always worked of course. Dad would love that sort of thing, and used to tease us about not being allowed to get ice cream because if he could not have any, then we should not be allowed any. If we got any, Dad would say, "Wait until I get up there! Next time I see you three, I will slap the back of your legs raw!", he would roar. Of course, it was all in jest. It made us all laugh so much. We would always send him a photo of us with the ice cream or just a simple photo of the ice cream itself to make sure he was very aware that we had ice cream, and that he was definitely not getting any. If he were messaging my Mum in the morning while she was on her way here, he would give her a stern warning that ice cream was not on the cards for us, as well as asking Mum to give me a great big hug from him.

We would lie out in the botanical gardens for hours on end, as they have toilets there, so that was my mum sorted. Her nickname in our family is 'pishy arse'. She always needed a pee; my Mum could never go without needing a pee for any length of time, so much so, it was highly brought up at her funeral. You had to plan your trips around what toilet facilities were available near each place because my mother always had to pee. There was never a single time I can remember her not having to pee when we went somewhere. If we walked to someone's house, she needed to pee, if we walked to Asda, the first thing she had to do was pee. Restaurant, had to pee; I think you get the gist by now. The botanical gardens were a great place to go after we had done a good gym session, then went on our way to enjoy the heat and the sun. We spent the day there or at the Clyde side. We would then go home and assess who had the worst sunburn before we started the dinner debate. Mum never ever knew what she wanted me to make, except that it would be chicken. Never how she wanted it cooked or what she wanted with it, just that she wanted chicken. We usually had a nice healthy chicken, rice, and vegetable combo of some variety. Then it was off to home for Mum right after dinner. Generally so quick, that the few times when my auntie Kellz would join us for dinner, she would comment on the fact that my Mum had barely finished swallowing her last bite before she had her jacket on, her pee done, and a foot out the door all at the same time. Sometimes she would get up and leave while we were all still eating! That was the way of my Mum; if she knew she could make the train then she was getting that train by hook or by crook.

Over the course of the next few months, things were pretty much back to normal for Mum and me. I went back to my work in July, as the lockdown was officially over at that point. Mum was back to coming to see me every single week again, never missing her Monday ritual. We had to wait on the gym opening, as they took much longer to reopen after lockdown; I think it was August before Mum and I could finally go. When we did get to go, we had to be extremely cautious as Mum had COPD. Unfortunately, you cannot control those around you who did not follow the rules. Mum wore her mask the entire time she was in the place, which to be fair, I was delightfully glad about, but it could not have been nice for her. This virus had really separated the stupidity of humanity from the ones with a willingness to survive, or certainly those who had not lost or felt they had nothing to lose. This is mostly what life consisted of for Mum and me pre and post-pandemic. Our days together were similar, but no less special in either of our eyes.

Chapter 4

Stephen Dying

Stephen's death came as a real shock to my system. I realise I am taking you back over what I have already covered, but I am trying to show you it from Mum's perspective. However, I know this book is supposed to be about my point of view, my feelings, and my thought process, which is why I feel the need to go over this again.

Stephen and I are cousins; his mum Angie and my Mum are sisters. We were close when we were kids, we drifted in our teen years, then Stephen and I became closer again as adults. When he was going through his divorce, I had also been going through a breakup from a six-year relationship with my fiancé at the time. Stephen and I found solace in one another. We often went for dinner and drinks to feel a lot less alone in this world, and in what we were going through at the time. We empowered each other and made each other very aware that we would get through this mess and life would indeed be good again. He was right, and we both did get through it and out the other side. I always knew that if I ever needed anything, Stephen would have dropped everything and come to my aid. That is just who he was; a good soul who would have done the same for anyone. As we got older, again we drifted apart, but he knew and I knew we would both be there if either of us needed the other.

He was diagnosed with cancer; skin cancer. It seemed to take a long time for the doctors to come to this conclusion, resulting in it spreading. He had to have amputations. In the beginning, it was just a toe, then more toes, then his foot, and then eventually from the knee down. There was hope they had removed it all at this point, but unfortunately, they did not, and it had spread on the inside this time. He found a lump in his groin area, and that was it really. From what I could tell from those closest to him, he knew when he found that lump his life was coming to an end. When I said his death was a shock to me, I can understand you may be thinking, how can it be a shock? He had cancer and you knew. Yes, I suppose you are right, we did know he had cancer. However, we did not expect him to go downhill so fast at that point. As far as we were all aware, he was ok for the moment and never in my mind did I ever think Stephen was going to die during the pandemic. This pandemic has been so, well… shit! It has taken so much from us and that is not even including the lives it has taken from us all. On the 21st of April, we were told he had 48 hours to live; he had been rushed into the hospital and that was it. I recall my Auntie Lynne calling me to give me the news. I was in shock. All I could think was please do not die during this pandemic, PLEASE NO! I could only think of him dying alone and how he would have no one with him due to the restrictions on the hospitals at the time. No family were allowed to be with him. He was alone.

This is the last thing you want for anyone. I remember thinking it was more likely to have been my Mum or Dad who would have been the ones to die during this pandemic. It was not fair for him to die during this whole thing, especially if it was not even from this stupid disease that was killing everyone already. I remember thinking of Italy, and seeing on tv that families could not be there to bury their loved ones, and how naive myself and the rest of this country had been to think 'that would not be us'. We would somehow avoid all of that. Well, boy, were we wrong. I guess it is not fair to say naïve; I was more hopeful it would not be as bad here somehow. Yeah, maybe naive is the right term. You just don't think it is going to happen to you. I was just too preoccupied thinking my Mum or Dad would get the virus, they are both already so ill that they might die. I didn't stop to think that anyone else could die from a different illness.

On the 22nd Stephen was on 100% oxygen. This, from my experience of death, is a sure-fire sign that you are not long for this earth. The reaper is standing in your doorway, ready to come at any moment, take your hand and lead the way. I remember sitting in my house feeling hopeless. I could not do anything; I could not go and be with my family which we would always do in these circumstances. We were always together in times like this. I felt glad that the pandemic had not hit Scotland as bad and that my Aunt Angie, Uncle James, his sister Jamie Marie, and brother Kevin got to be there with him when he passed away. I felt grateful knowing he was not alone in death. I have no idea what it is like to die, but I have seen rather a few people in my time take their last breath, and I cannot imagine a soul wanting to be alone in those moments. I think having people there to cheer you on your way to wherever it is our energy ends up is something we all should long for. I admire any nurse or doctor who sits with a patient when they are alone in death to take that loneliness away, lifting the fear for them. These people are saints! That is someone you know has seen so much death, they understand it is not a time to be alone for anyone. So, I was grateful Stephen got to go towards his end with his family with him, that they all got to say goodbye and so did he. That is all you can want for a person and their family. However, I was in a house with no one who even knew Stephen at all. I felt so alone and unattached to the world. I lived the furthest away from everyone in our family as well. I was so far from Mum and all I wanted was my Mum! I just wanted to see her, be with her, and for her to make me feel better as only your Mum really can. I am sorry to anyone reading this who had to endure life without a mum. I could not begin to imagine what that must have been like for you until now my Mum has gone from me. The feeling of absolute helplessness in a time the world is upside down is one I think so many can relate to, to be honest. I think most of you reading this will be able to relate to this feeling at some point or other, whether the reason be big or small. That feeling of inability at some period during 2020, being unable to do things for people you love; tasks that would normally be effortless.

My auntie Lynne had been calling me a lot at that time to make sure I was ok. I had told her it did not matter the hour of the day, but that I wanted her to let me know Stephen had passed when it came. I remember not being able to sleep for days and then the one night when I did finally fall asleep, it just so happened to be the night he passed. At 2:22 AM my Auntie Lynne called. She said, "Sweetheart, I am so sorry, but Stephen passed away.". She asked if I could call my Mum and let her know as she didn't have her number. I could not even take in the news myself as I had not fully woken up yet, but I immediately called my Mum. She did not answer at first, so I called her house as I knew she would know something was wrong that way. She answered sounding tired and faded on the phone. I said, "Mum, are you awake?"

She replied, "Aye, hen, what's wrong?"

I said, "Mum, I am so sorry, but Stephen has died. I have just got off the phone to Auntie Lynne.". My Mum could not really believe it herself.

I explained he had not been on his own in this. He was with family, and that Auntie Angie, Uncle James, Jaime Marie, and their brother Kevin all got to be there with him and that is what was important. He was not alone. He had family there with him. Mum took comfort in that, and we spoke for a little while as she woke up a bit more. At that point, we knew nothing about what would happen for his funeral, so Mum and I spoke of not being able to imagine what this must be like for Auntie Angie and Uncle James. What we thought would happen, given the rules, with Stephen's funeral in terms of numbers and a wake. Then I said goodnight to Mum. I did not sleep a wink the rest of the night. I messaged my best friend at the time to tell him about it, apologising for the hour but that I thought he would want to know. Matthew knew as he was next to me when the phone rang. He had fallen back to sleep fast as he had been up with me the prior few nights. It was a constant discussion in the house for the next while, Stephen and the situation he was in, and what would happen with his funeral. The pandemic was taking basic human needs away from those around me. We were thinking about the number of people who did have to die alone, and how my family was at least lucky that Nicola Sturgeon (Scotland's first minister) took better care of our country faster so that Stephen did not end up dying alone. But I really felt so terribly isolated by his passing.

I have never really felt grief like it myself. I think the fact we were scared to even go for the one walk a day that we were allowed did not help. As human beings, sharing your pain is one of the best things you can do and denying us that is awful, even while it is understandable at the time. For me, I deal better if I am able to help others with their pain using my past experiences to guide them to a better understanding of their thoughts and feelings, hence my need to write this book. I do my best to keep it together for those around me like Mum, or anyone really. I learned pretty young that I had to be the so-called 'man' of my household, and when shit hit the fan I needed to be tearless, strong, and brave for Mum. Turned out, she needed me more than I needed her in many ways. This time I was not able to be there for anyone. I received lots of messages with words of strength and courage when Stephen died. These were things I already knew and fully understood, but these people were simply trying to help me. The thing about death is that at the beginning of it, there are no words that anyone can say to you that will help at all. I know that nothing you can say will help a person in their immediate feelings of loss. There is nothing wrong with simply saying to a person you don't know what to say and keeping your words of encouragement for a little later, when they are more equipped to hear it from you. When the dust has settled and things have moved on a little in their minds, then tell them all those things you were going to tell them at the start.

The lesson I have learned most about death is that you will certainly know who cares, who does not care at all, and who is simply pretending to care for you. These things become very apparent extremely quickly. Almost everyone will fade away at a time when you feel you need them the most. This is not their fault, as life moves on even when yours seems at a standstill. This became more apparent to me with Mum dying rather than with Stephen. Still, messages are nice to have from people with words of support and kindness at a time when you are suffering. It is the messages from people you do not get that becomes so very apparent and alarming. The people you assumed should and would message you and did not bother. Not even an, "I am sorry," or, "I do not know what to say." Nothing, maybe even a simple, "hope you are ok," or, "If you need to talk let me know.". People you have known for years or people you have helped say nothing to you at all. I have never quite understood this to be honest with you. It seems excessively bizarre to me that some people cannot muster up a message. I get that most of us have things going on in our lives, but it takes but a simple second to write any of the things I have said above. Even if you do not like a person, you should never wish death upon someone's life and you should certainly address the death by expressing that you are sorry to hear about the news, ask how they are doing, and so on. I would love to ask some of the people who I think should have sent me kind regards why they did not or could not, so I can gain understanding on this. I cannot imagine it would go down well though, and I would not want anyone to be made feel bad for something. I guess maybe they could not bring themselves to do it or had good reasoning for not saying anything. Maybe these people actually do have great reasons for it; I would just like to really gain an understanding of it.

The day Stephen died I was so lost in myself, my mind felt like it was up in space a little. Messaging family members to make sure they were ok, expressing my feeling of just pure hopelessness in being this far away from everyone. I knew a lot of them had been able to see each other or be near each other. I felt so lost and alone. I had not experienced the anger yet, that would not come for a while - actually around Matthew's birthday time. Now, just a sense of loss and hopelessness. I was not getting out of my bed really, I was sleeping a lot, not really having a care in the world and the best part was because we were in lockdown, no one was able to really notice. Which, at the time, felt like the best thing for me when in actuality it was extremely damaging. A sense of darkness had taken over me, one I had not felt for many years, not since trying to take my own life a few years prior. It was an extremely dark and horrible time. Being able to go to the funeral and at least say goodbye was good for me. It gave me a sense of closure. I do not think I understood just how down I was at the time until reflecting upon it now. I am the type of person who likes to get up and go, needs a sense of purpose. Lockdown hit me hard, as well as everyone else. I signed up to be a volunteer to fill my days, but during the entirety of lockdown, I received one call, not an ideal situation for me.

Dealing with everything from the Mum and John situation, to then dealing with Stephen dying was honestly a rather huge blow to my perspective. I had been getting out in the sun and trying to make an effort, but on the inside, I felt awful and numb. Just a seeping hole inside of me, sucking all my happiness away. This sounds like depression, and I am sure if I had visited a doctor he would have confirmed it was depression. Yet, I do not think it was depression at all; I think it was life. It is a part of life to experience these thoughts and emotions, and I think it is in our ability to identify them and understand how to fix them that will better us all in the end. If I had been to a doctor, I could have easily picked up some antidepressants; I have been offered them many times throughout my years. But I have never taken them once. I passionately believe they are a short-term solution to a long-term problem. They are not something a single soul on earth should be allowed to become dependent on. They are not forever, nor should they ever be allowed to be. They are to help you in your darkest moments, and then you learn to help yourself from there as you come off them.

I want everyone on this earth to understand that everyone has or will feel the way you feel in these moments right now. You are not alone, and I will repeat that in this book as many times as I need to for the thought to sink in. You are more than capable of helping yourself out of your darkest places. You need to be genuinely willing to get out of that dark place you are allowing yourself to be in. I am saying this from first-hand experience with a hard, troubled life and with first-hand experience with someone who had severe depression.

Stephen dying was awful, but I got over it because I wanted to, because I had the will to get out the other side of it. I will do the same with Mum dying. There is no such thing as never getting over it or that things will never be the same. I see all the time from *those* people on social media that it does not get any easier, a statement I absolutely hate and refuse to ever get behind. Everything in life can get easier if you are willing to let it. If it is not getting easier for you in that moment, this is because you do not want it to get easier. You are clinging to the pain and the sadness; you need to want to let that go.

I think a lot of people believe this is how you honour the dead. I personally think that is an insult to their memory. Do you really think someone who loved you during their life wants *your* whole life to come to a complete standstill when they die? Because I certainly do not! I think to cling to the pain you are feeling is selfish. You are making someone else's death about you. You did not die, they did. Of course, you should be sad they are gone but do not sit there for years in self-pity trying to find something or someone to blame for it all. Get up and honour that person by living the best life you possibly can. Nothing is certain, and tomorrow is never promised to us, so go out there and make the absolute most of the small amount of time we have on this earth. Being here with the ability to think and feel is a gift in itself, so cherish it and use it in the best way you know how to.

My cousin Stephen was thirty-five when he died, had not long turned it either! Thirty-five! He did not want to die; he was taken, and unfortunately it was cruel and left a mother and father having to bury their child. I can assure you now if Stephen could be brought back tomorrow to tell us all something, he would say get the fuck up and make the most of the life you have, this air you get to breathe. Go out and seize the moment and feel the sun on your face like you have never

ever felt it before. Experiencing all the feelings that come with death is so important, but so is letting them all go again. They are not there to be clung to. They are there to be fleeting and essential to your growth as a human being.

Why would you want to cling to sadness? Think about that for a second. Really, please stop reading, pop the book down, and take a moment. Why do I feel the need to hold on to sadness and pain? Where has that come from?

Now come back to me with your answer. Was it because it is what you have seen others do around you? Parents, maybe? Their parents? Do we think we must do as we have seen? Are we born to think that way? No, we are not. We choose to hold on to the things we hold on to. Can I plead with you now to try and stop doing it? It will not be easy, but you need to learn to let these things go. As I said, pain should be a fleeting feeling that comes around to help us grow. For a lot of us, it comes around to stunt our growth and we get trapped inside it. Learn to talk in the moment of pain and suffering, learn to write it down, learn to set it on fire, learn to meditate, whatever it is that helps you feel that weight lift off of your shoulders. Do it!

Go out and make your life that little bit brighter; do it for you. Do it because you deserve a better, happier life, and so does your husband, wife, kids, family, and friends. You cannot give your best to someone if you have never felt your best for yourself.

Chapter 5

Losing My Best Friend

To be honest with you, I do not know how to begin to describe this to you and I think by the end you will understand why. I have had my best friend in my life for many years now. He was my maid of honour at my wedding last year in 2019. We have been through so much together. Yet, he decided to call it a day for what honestly seemed like the worst reason I can think of, which I will go into in more detail. After Stephen died, I mentioned I was not in a good mental state at all. I did not keep this from my best friend; in fact, I was really open and honest about it.

I understand that you are only getting my side of this story, but I will tell it as fairly as I can, and I can obviously only give my point of view here, and tell you what he said to me. To be honest, he did not give me much closure, nor did he give me any reasons or good explanations as to the real reason he decided to stop being my friend. It seemed to me that he made something up quickly in an attempt to silence my questioning. I am also only telling you of this from a grief point of view; this is not to make anyone look bad.

It started from me being in a bad place, which I was, and always was very open about. Talking about our mental state is one of the best ways to actually begin to process it and rationalise the reasoning behind why you feel the way you feel. I have come across so many young adults as well as many older people who do not understand this. I think the reason I am good at it is from years of dealing with a lot of pent-up feelings, anger, and years of watching my Mum struggle with everything, knowing I did not want to become like her; well, not the bad parts of her. There are loads of my Mum's traits that I strived to emulate and have become because she is and was amazing. She was my wonder woman. She taught me the beginnings of feminism and equality among genders by teaching me skills that men would usually be known to do. She taught me how to be independent, to not need men to get through life.

Back to the point. So, in the May time frame, I was freaking out a little, due to it being Matthew's 30th soon. I knew he would need to spend his 30th in lockdown. I was and am very aware that is hardly the worst thing to ever happen to anyone. It is rubbish, none the less though. Sometimes you need the good to help outweigh the bad, and I think with my cousin dying I was always so aware that any moment can be your last moment, so I was trying everything I could to make this a great birthday for him. Trying to arrange for people to come over and see him outside of the house, as loads of people had done similar things throughout lockdown, keeping a safe distance from us and them; it's just nice to see a face or two that you had not seen for a while. I was trying to arrange for as many people as I could to pop over if they drove, so they were not using public transport. We could talk to them if they rolled down their window and not pick up the nasty virus; plus, at that point, none of us had seen anyone for months.

Matthew's birthday is in June, so a good while after Stephen's funeral which was the last time I had been around anyone, and Matthew couldn't go to that. I had tried to get Matthew's mum to come over but she really didn't' want to risk it; I was trying to persuade her to do it for Matt's sake. If she did not come over, he would not see any of his family at all for his birthday which I thought was really sad. For all any of us know, this could be their last or yours; either way, I feel it's just important to try and celebrate. The fact Stephen had just died made it more apparent that we need to try and cherish every moment we can. I have experienced a lot of death in my lifetime from such a young age. I would say Matthew and his family have been really fortunate in the sense that they haven't had to deal with that, so I can kind of relate to them not understanding my viewpoint here. I was grieving though, and annoyed because she did not want to see her own son on his thirtieth. My Mum was not like that with us; she would have walked to be with us on our thirtieth, she would have died for us, and in fact, I think she did die for me.

Matthew's mum was worried about getting a fine. I was trying to ease her mind with that. I was aware that virtually everyone at this point was not giving a hoot about the rules. I had seen on Facebook and Instagram that people were gathering in large groups indoors and in all sorts of places. I knew she would make it over without getting a fine. I was getting annoyed easily though because I was not myself; I was in a dark place. I snapped at her a little. I went to my best friend and auntie for advice about it. I wanted to know their honest opinion on it as you do – did they think I was right, or was I being out of line? I am always like this; I will always ask for an outside perspective to make sure I am not being irrational, especially when I know I have had something major happen. I knew my best friend had broken the rules a few times himself, so I wanted to know what he thought. I like to ask people these things so you can really get advice about your mindset from someone you trust.

I asked Kellz and she said I was obviously overly emotional in the moment, but she did not think I was wrong. Whereas when I asked my best friend, he said, "I'd rather not comment," which I found to be so very odd. So, I pushed him on it and explained I wanted his honest opinion as he had often given me in the past, many times, in fact. To which, by the way, I welcome criticism. I do not mind it at all, especially if I have gone out of my way to ask for it. You may be sitting there thinking I was in the wrong too, and that is totally fine. We are all allowed our own opinions about everything in this life. I was expecting something from him; anything but 'no comment'. He decided to tell me something along the lines of you *should* be able to give your friend your opinions. Sharing his opinion with me was something he definitely could and had done before, and I haven't lost my head in any way nor have I taken it poorly. I may have tried to give my point of view a little more strongly to help him have understanding, but to tell me you cannot give me your opinion if you think I am wrong, is definitely wrong!

After thinking about it I said to him, maybe with haste and irrational thinking, that maybe we should not be friends anymore. At this point, I was still in my bed, halfway through the day where I had been for days on end. Definitely in a slight depression, a full-on funk about life, death, and everything in between. So, I acted super-irrationally, which if you have not been through losing someone yet, will happen to you. You can really become someone else entirely for a while because you allow yourself to fall into a slump of depression without meaning to or realising it. I have to say that losing someone so important in your life is really hard too, especially a friend. I have found this to greatly upset my chi anytime it has happened to me throughout the years. Losing a good friend is like going through a full breakup. It really is awful; it makes you question so much about yourself and them. What did you miss? What could you have done better? Should you be fighting to keep them? Even if you did fight to keep them and they stayed, would it be the same after that point? Could you two carry on through life the same way you always had? Would you now be forever questioning your ability to be a good friend? Just so many things to think about, and the list is longer than those I have stated.

He then decided, even after me apologising and explaining I was being an idiot, that he did not want to be friends anymore. It was very clear he had been waiting for this moment for a while, and the opportunity had come along, I had given him an out. I have no idea why he felt he needed this out, to be honest. His explanation was that we had become too co-dependent, which makes no sense at all. We definitely had not, but even if we had, that's surely what friendship is all about, is it not? About relying on another person to be there for you in a time of need? Asking a friend for his opinion on a matter is not co-dependency; I personally think that is called friendship.

However, at the end of the day, despite how torn up I was about it, he had to do what is right for him. Maybe my things were just too much for him to handle; maybe we just were not in the right places at the right times for him to cope with. Maybe the fact lockdown was happening drove this. There are so many maybes and justifiable reasons for it. However, it did not make it hurt any less. More so because I could tell from how he was acting towards me immediately after it; it was like a switch had flipped and he had become another person. Not the guy I knew for sure; my husband also could not believe or understand the change in his attitude towards me. It was odd to say the least. I was devastated. In one of those times and moments when I thought I was losing everything around me, it really was not a good feeling to lose someone who stood by you not even a full year before and signed your wedding document. I personally felt he knew before then that he did not want to be my friend. I had not noticed it until he said it, but there were signs that I should have noticed; maybe I simply did not want to notice. Maybe I just wanted to get through my wedding without a hiccup, as anyone does. Our wedding was absolutely amazing and did go off without a hitch.

I definitely went through the full five stages of grieving over my best friend's decision to not be my friend anymore; I cried about it, got angry, tried bargaining, was in denial, and dealt with depression before finally accepting the fact. It took me months; in fact, I do not think I fully accepted it until my Mum died. That is when I knew it was done for good, when he knew the details of my Mum's funeral, and did not show his face. Which he should have; he knew my Mum of his own right. He did her shopping during lockdown for her, they had their own relationship without me. His family supported me through Mum dying, but not him. It was then that I really thought, "Wow!" This really was the end of our friendship. To not come to Mum's rosary or funeral was truly hurtful. I told him Mum had died because I thought he deserved to know, due to him knowing my Mum so well over the years.

This is the same reason I told my best friend from primary school, even though she and I are not close now, but she came to Mum's funeral irrespective because that is what you do. She was at the graveyard to show her support for me and for my Mum, as she too had her own separate relationship with her. So, in that moment, I knew I was done with him too and it was over because I do not need someone in my life who cannot support me in serious times like these. I felt by not attending any of the proceedings for Mum's funeral, he was slamming the door shut.

The pain is unbelievable when a friend decides to no longer be your friend. If this has ever happened to you, then you do know pain, and you do know grief. I can imagine this to have happened to everyone at least once in their lives. As I stated, he was right to do that if he felt he needed to for himself. Absolutely! It does not stop it from hurting like hell though. You are entitled to feel your feelings, all of them, as of and when you need to. Talk about them often, it really does help if you lay them all out and see them in order. Speaking it out helps rationalise the thought process and gain an understanding of it all. After seeking advice from others around me, they also did not think his explanation seemed right. It was too vague and out of the blue. I just wish him well and to be happy in all his endeavours in this life.

So, that was another great part of this *fantastic* year.

Chapter 6

Back in Time

I am going to take you back in time now for a while; then I will bring you back to 2020. I will start from the beginning. Well -- from my beginning. I was born in October 1990, back in the day when parents did not really find out about the pregnancy or gender. My Mum's description of the day I was born explains her feeling toward it very well. She used to say, "When you came out after hours and hours of labour, all I could see was your bum in the air. But then you opened your legs, and I could see that the crack went the full way around. I was absolutely thrilled." She had always wanted a little girl, and she had got one. My Dad also wanted a girl too, so I think they were both over the moon.

I do not recall the first few years of my life so; I only have what I was told to go on. I believe though, that life was not full of happiness and hope. My Mum always had a drinking problem, but she was younger then, and I do not think anyone identified it as a drinking problem, but it definitely was. Dad was a gambler; we were not rich by any means at all. My Mum would have been a full-time mum when I was born. She was then a part-time cleaner in Columba High School in Coatbridge, where we lived. Coatbridge itself is not the nicest of places to live. Dad was working with my uncle as an assistant to him while he was a painter and decorator, so we were not exactly overly wealthy or even slightly wealthy. I grew up in a terraced council house at 92 Daldowie St, Kirskshaws. That was the place I was born into; later, we would find out that Kirkshaws was an awful place to live. But it definitely built my character, in some ways I'd rather forget.

I can certainly claim that my childhood wasn't a happy one most of the time. My Mum and Dad fought often about so many things; they were cruel and horrible to each other throughout the short time they were together in my life. I had an older brother; Paul Patrick Gallacher. He is exactly five years older than me, also born in October, but in 1985. As far as Mum led me to believe, over the years my Dad was not a good man. He was abusive to her and did not give us a good time, either. I personally do not recall any of this at all, as I was so young.

My Mum did tell me the tale of the first time I may have reported to her I was abused though. She said that one day I had come in when I was two-ish saying Paul had touched me in a place he should not have. I believe they did not think much of it at the time. However, with my recollection of it, as parts have come back to me over the years, I was forever getting cream on my 'little flower,' as I called it. Every night and day, I can remember lying on my carpet in my living room to get my cream on, because I was always red and inflamed in the southern parts. I remember my um always thinking how so very odd it was. I cannot to this day recall any abuse from that age, but I do remember other parts as I get older. For many years, I went through my life remembering nothing before I was about ten unless it was really a big thing in my life. One time I fainted in my kitchen, I remember that, or I fell over the handlebars of my bike, and I remember that. Otherwise, it was all a big blank; everything, the good, the bad, did not matter, I could not remember a thing about any of it.

When I was four years old, my Dad either left us or was kicked out, depending on who you talk to. There is a rumour that Paul was not actually my Dad's child (Dad is aware of this, he is not going to read this and find out). A large part of me has hoped it is true, but we will never know now. This seems to be the real reason he left, although Mum had always made it out vastly different to us as kids. She did not like it much if we wanted to be with Dad, which I can understand to an extent. Keep in mind, I told you my Mum has definitely had mental health issues since she was a very young girl. I am not saying it justifies all her actions by any means, but it does certainly explain them over the years to come. Mum and Dad seemed to split up amicably at first, but as time went on it turned on its head. I think for most people who get divorced this tends to happen, especially when kids are involved. It ended up a pissing contest really; unfortunately, Paul and I were caught in the crossfire of it all. Dad was allowed visitation while the divorce was happening. If I remember right, it was on Wednesdays and Saturdays; these are probably still standard to this day. I have and never will understand why a man's rights are not equivalent to those of a woman. It is actually so backwards, it is unbelievable. Dad was always there at the start to pick us up and take us for the day. Then that started to fade away. He lived with my Mum's sister Angie, her husband James, and their three kids after he left us. We would go up there to see Dad, and Uncle James would give him a lift to pick us up and drop us off.

I clearly remember one time, one of the kids saying to Paul and me "Ha, ha, your daddy lives with us and not you.". Now, we were all kids and they did not mean it how we as adults would take that now. However, let me assure you that that cut me to the bone. It was like someone took my heart out and replaced it with an ice cube, while they kicked me in the stomach at the same time. It is wildly funny how even though I was only four I remember that, and I doubt I will ever forget it to be honest. Something that causes us pain is stored for our own protection in the future. Now I do not hold a grudge about that at all, nor do I hold grudges in general; it is not my style. I do, however, have a great memory because I have been hurt and abused and I can read people exceptionally well. I can do that because I have the memory of all the little events like this, that did hurt me over the years, to help protect me from being hurt by people again. I can usually read people's character exceptionally well. I will steer clear of anyone who I think will cause me unnecessary pain or hurt.

It got to a point my Dad would stop showing up and we would be waiting at the window for him for hours on end, hoping he would show up. The pain of him not showing up was unbelievable as a child; you are so naïve, hopeful, and have so much faith in humanity and the world that you do not think anyone can let you down so badly. I can remember my Mum going on about this a lot. She would bring up how she hated seeing us sitting by the window watching for him, having to deal with us wondering why our Dad did not love us enough to come and see us. As an adult now and even when I hit maybe sixteen or seventeen, I realised that all is not as simple as it seems. There are two sides to every story, and one day maybe I will hear my Dad's side of all of this. It was great for Mum in the sense that she did not want us to want my Dad. Yet, the more he did not turn up, the more we longed for him. I gave up very quickly, but I was incredibly young and had spent less time with my Dad than Paul had. Paul never lost his need for my Dad, and my Mum could never ever understand it.

My Dad was the punisher of us all, and I come from a generation where hitting your kids was allowed and legal. So, my Dad battered Paul from time to time. Paul was trouble, and I think he was a LOT of trouble after I was born. He was a child with extensive jealousy issues. He never liked me as a baby. He did not understand why I got attention and he did not. As far as I can tell from both my Mum and my Dad, Paul would go out of his way to make me cry as a kid, hurting me or annoying me because he did not like me at all, so he would get a sore bum for it. Which, again he did not like, and as Paul got older his habits got worse. He stole from people, lied all the time, opened his mouth to the wrong people at school or when he was out playing in the street. Mum could never understand why he would want my Dad when it was my Dad who was the punisher of the family. Mum also had this extreme need to feel needed by those around her. She needed the validation; I think due to her insecurities.

She used to shout at Paul for wanting my Dad, which I think is sad really. Mainly because I understand, and understood that want my whole life. If you are reading this as a grown-up in a two-parent family, you will hopefully have no idea what I am talking about. However, if you are reading this and one of your parents left and never came back or passed away when you were young, then you know exactly what I am talking about. In fact, if you have been adopted you will also know what I speak of. It is hard to not want to know the people who birthed you. It seems to me after research, years of experience, and talking to people, there is a biological instinct to want to know them for us homo sapiens. I could never help this feeling of wonder about my Dad, and where he was and what was he doing. Did I look like him; was I like him? I never thought I could be like a person who didn't raise me, but it turns out I was actually very much like my Dad in so many ways, even without knowing him. I

GRIEF

remember my Mum telling me 'you are just like your father!', trying to hurt me of course at the time or in the moment, but she didn't hurt me at all, because in my head I was thinking, "How on earth can I be like a man I don't know and had no impact on my life?". Yet, I really am like my Dad in so many ways, and I can see now why Mum preferred Paul to me. It might also be to do with the fact that Paul was perhaps not my Dad's child. Since I was and she did not like my Dad, but she did like whomever Paul's dad was, then it is appropriate to conclude that she would have resentment towards me.

I will never forget the day Dad brought his new girlfriend Lorraine and her son Michael to our house on one of the days he was visiting us. It was truly one of the most heart-wrenching days I have had in my young life. Seeing your dad with another child who is not you is possibly the most horrifying thing to feel at five years old. The sense that he was gone and now he had a new family sat with me uneasily; it caused me to have serious anxiety as a child about my Mum ever leaving me. There was one time as a kid my Auntie Lynne was trying to take my Mum out for a wee night out. I think she hadn't had a night out in years at this point, due to being a single parent. My gran and grandad were babysitting Paul and I, and when Mum got up to leave, I literally started screaming my head off. Which may seem like I am being a brat to most, but I most definitely was not. I thought my Mum was not coming back, the same way my Dad did not come back one day. That fear for a child is something you cannot begin to imagine unless you went through it. I have nothing as an adult that is comparable, not even my Mum dying.

Dad had brought Michael and Lorraine with him to Mum's house to pick us up, and as you can imagine, he did not tell Mum he was doing it, so when they showed up her face was a picture. I can understand her anger; she had no time to prepare Paul and I for this new woman, never mind her son, who we obviously automatically hated! It was only natural to feel that way about it. I remember Michael was at my Auntie Angie's wedding with his mother Lorraine. We were there with our Mum, of course, Michael came up to Paul and I and was saying our Dad was his dad. As you can imagine, I thought Paul was going to literally murder this child. Michael was younger than me at the time and he obviously did not mean to hurt us at all, but he also did not understand when Paul and I were saying to him; "No, he is our Dad, Michael, not yours!". Paul was already a bit of a lost cause by this point in his life, so he was ready to kill this kid. Not Michael's fault, of course, but still not ours either. We were all kids.

My Dad was a massive gambler which led to our already-poor existence being even poorer. I know he used to use money set aside for bills to gamble, and we would not have enough for day-to-day things. It was not the ideal set up for marriage. They only got married in the first place so they could christen Paul, as good old religion would not allow a baptism if they were not married. I am not a big fan of religion, so sorry if you are, but it is not for me. They got married for all the wrong reasons and then had me to add to the equation, which I cannot imagine helped what was already a recipe for disaster. With the drinking, the gambling, Mum's mental health, and so on, they both had a lot of issues to work on. Neither had been raised in a world that equipped you to be better able to deal with your issues, nor did it raise them about the empowerment of healing; they were taught to not deal with anything.

My Dad had to be a *man* and Mum was taught to sweep it all under the carpet. No real ability was given to them to help themselves. Nothing like what you have in the world today; even I am old enough to have been in the world before all the self-help and self-love became a big thing. It is an amazing thing, and I wish all generations had access to this knowledge.

GRIEF

Maybe then there would not have been so much bad blood between people and families alike. An ability to talk openly about ourselves, our feelings, and fear is one of the most powerful things we have. I have learned that myself over the years. Their marriage was crumbling. I do not think anything they could have done would have saved it. Dad was silly when it came to not thinking about what his actions did to hurt those around him, especially bringing Michael to our house like that. Dad left for England at some point when I was five or six and we never saw him again. He went away with Lorraine and Michael. The next we heard of him, he had apparently had a daughter with her named Carla who, according to her mother, was my spitting image…except she looked nothing like me at all! I had black hair and brown eyes with sallow skin, whereas she had blonde hair, blue eyes, and was chalk white. Nothing like me or my Dad.

Mum and Dad had Paul when Mum was twenty-one and Dad was twenty-five. I feel this to be very young to have a baby. I used to think in my life I would have a plan, and I would be married by twenty-five, and babies by twenty-seven because society taught me that that was how it needed to be, but now I realise I do not even want to have babies at all. Matthew and I would love to adopt a child after we have travelled a lot more and do the things we want to do in life. You do not need to follow the status quo; you can do what makes you happy. There are plenty of people on this planet procreating and there are also plenty of children needing a good home to go to. I would beg and urge anyone to reconsider having babies and think about adopting one. Maybe in years to come, I can write another book about my experiences with adoption, so people can have a better understanding of it too.

Having babies young seems to be an important factor in what tends to break up marriages and relationships in years to come, because as you get older and more mature you realise there was so much you wanted to do in your life, and having that little baby really held you back; then people seem to question the whys. Whose idea was it to have a baby anyway? Did they even want that? Then the resentment builds up. For Mum and Dad, this was not necessarily the case, I just feel it is for so many people out there. I would conclusively say that society taught my parents that they had to stay together for as long as they could, even if it wasn't right. This is another thing their generation seemed to get wrong, raising kids in an unhappy household and thinking you should stay together for them is so wrong. You cause the kids so much pain and they do not even realise that is the reason for their pain. They are better off having separated parents and have happy parents rather than living in a house filled with hate.

Chapter 7

Being Mum and Dad

Mum became a single parent on benefits after dad left; life was always tough on benefits. We never had any spare cash for anything at all. Mum spent the money she did get wisely (except she smoked, not the best investment) on the things we needed and liked as best she could. I cannot imagine being my mum and having to take all of that on, on her own.

I wrote on Facebook last year for Mother's Day:

Happy Mother's Day, Mum! I love you unconditionally!

You are an extremely special human to me! There are so, so, so many people today who will be giving it "aww, my perfect Mum!" Blah, blah and I just want to say to you, Mum, thanks for not making it perfect, because life is not about perfect! Life is about dealing with the hardest stuff the right way and using those moments as teachable lessons to make me tougher and stronger! That is what you did, Mum, and now that the world Is currently falling to pieces, I am able to handle that. That's because of you, Mum!

I will never be able to thank you enough for making me so tough and resilient, yet also lovable and emotional. Thanks for showing me the beauty of all things even though at times you may forget it yourself!

Thanks for also helping me understand that with beauty also comes horror, and that although horror at the time is devastating, it also helps harden our exterior and shape who we are going to be!

So yeah, thanks, Mary Hen! You are a true trooper! Xxxxx

Love you always x

My Mum really did not make it perfect at all, but in ways, she was my hero for sure. Mum really stepped up to the mark when it came to raising us on her own, I think. She became a bit of a wonder woman and taught herself how to do everything, including wallpapering, painting, laying carpets, and moving furniture. It really did not matter the task; she would have given it a go, that was for sure. She always made sure we had what we needed, maybe not what we wanted, but what we needed. She sorted everything on her own for us. Dedicated her life to us. Paul gave her such a hard time over the years with his lying, stealing, and hitting me. He gave her no peace.

Paul always had a big mouth and nothing to back it up. I remember one time before my Dad left, Paul was being bullied at St. James primary school. My Dad went to the school with Mum and I to see if what Paul was saying was true, so the three of us stood behind a wall and watched as this young boy tormented Paul. My Dad had seen enough; the boy had broken Paul's nose, so my Dad walked over and picked the wee guy up by the hair (no exaggeration) and dragged him straight to the head teacher's office. After that day, Paul ended up going to St. Mary's primary school in Whifflet.

Paul caused Mum and I a lot of grief over the years, especially when we lived in Kirkshaws. He just never ever learned to shut his mouth. I can always remember Paul trying to recruit me. That is what it was all about to Paul, somehow it was about him recruiting others into his ways of life. He was a rather messed-up human being.

Being a single mum of two must have been so hard for my Mum in the 90s. Mum comes from a large family, and none of us had a pot to piss in, as they say. There are nine in Mum's family, her mother and father (Mary + Alec), she also had five sisters and one brother (Catherine, Thomas, Angela, Lynne, Jacqueline, and Kellymarie). Kellymarie came along a few years after the rest of the clan. So, she did not actually grow up with them. She is six years older than me and twenty years younger than my Mum. A good Catholic family indeed, who had nothing growing up.

Whenever Mum made us dinner, she would give us a portion you would not believe because she was so used to having nothing between eight of them, therefore she never wanted us to go without. She gave you a potato mountain, not just some potatoes. I believe all my Mum ever tried to do was give us a better life than she had. I believe she succeeded in that, given what I knew about what their lives were like. *Only* having a mum was rather traumatic at times for us as kids, especially since 90% of our classmates still had their dad; not understanding why people would look at you funny if you told them your mum did not work as well. We were too young to understand that they thought we were beneath them; as an adult, I know now. I think if you ever look at a child that way you are filth! No child asks for the life they have. They are just trying to live a happy, carefree day if they can. The feeling people left us with as we got older and realised why they were looking at us in such a way was truly degrading. We did nothing wrong to be in the situation we were in, and for grown men and woman to look at us or judge us was unfair.

Christmases and birthdays were always a bad time for us and for Mum. Well, we loved it, but Mum usually cried during them because we did not have much and that killed her. She never intended her life to be as it was, but things happen and sometimes that is just how it goes. The worst of it was Mum adored Christmas. She was all for it and made us love it so much. I am still a huge fan of it today because she made us love it so much. The first of December was time to pop the tree up; it was always a great feeling, and she would get her vinyl of the Jive Bunny's Christmas remix out, dust it off, and pop it on for us. I still play it to this day to wake up my household on Christmas morning. It really is an excellent piece of Christmas cheer. She always tried her best for us at Christmas time, and I know if it were not for my gran, we would not have been as well off at Christmas or at birthdays either. My gran was our lifesaver most of the time. Mum adored my granny and rightly so; she was a mental 'wee Scottish woman' who tended to punch first and ask questions later. She was really something else, but for us, she had the biggest heart of them all. Well, we certainly felt that way. Even Paul would have run a thousand miles for Gran. I think he also knew without her it would not have been as good as it was.

We were the kids you went to school with that had the faded badge on their jumper, because we could not afford five new jumpers every year and some of ours were most likely hand-me-downs. My communion dress was my older cousin Nicola's because we were both distinctly tall for our age and for girls, both big skinny drinks of water as well. I think I got a lot of clothes from Nicola, we were really close as kids. Mum and Auntie Catherine (Nicola's mum) were close when we were growing up so. They were a huge part in shaping me and who I have become in my adult life.

Mum was burdened with having to be both parents to us. She had to be the good and the bad, the hope and the fear, the pain and the light for us. I cannot begin to imagine what a single mother has to go through. I do not ever want to find out either, as it is not something anyone seeks out. There were times we had Mum at her wit's end. Paul and I could be a handful; we were boisterous and into wrestling, so we were always knocking lumps out of each other.

There was a story I have always loved from me and Paul, but it is not actually a lovable story, to be honest with you. Paul and I had woken up before Mum on the weekend, which was normal. We had decided to make cereal for ourselves, probably putting a mixture of all the cereals we had into one bowl because Mum would not know we had done it. Paul decided to throw a metal spoon at my head and he got me right on the forehead. Safe to say I was not amused by his success. I decided to go and fetch my Mum's umbrella, open it as if it was some sort of lightsaber, and run at Paul with it. Paul, for lack of more effective wording, was a "shite bag." He ran away from me with great haste. I caught up to him, though. He hid under his duvet as if somehow that would protect him from the great angry ball that was me. I lifted the umbrella and with all my might smashed it down into the duvet he lay under. I struck gold. He let out a roaring scream, which unfortunately Mum heard, and came running, I had belted him in the nose with it!

Much to Mum's disappointment, the umbrella did not survive. She was angrier I had now put a bend in the only umbrella she had than the fact I smacked Paul with it. Probably because Paul was unscathed, and her poor umbrella was a goner. There was no hope for the poor thing. I think Mum was of the mindset that Paul got what he deserved for hitting me with the spoon. I did not take well to bullies; I'm not sure if that's because I had to stand up to Paul for years. Funny how things change in you as you get older and life changes who you are. As a teen, I was so quiet and anxiety-filled, I would not have said boo to a goose. As a child, I was taking on the biggest guys on the street for Paul! I was also gifted with a family trait - I am very quick-witted. Anything they had to say I was ready for them, able to bring them down to nothing usually. It's not hard to be a bully; it usually entails a lack of intelligence. I cannot think for a second what that must have been like for Mum to have to deal with that as a single parent, suffering from depression, alcoholism (which she was always in denial about, until the day she died), and denial. She held a great deal on her shoulders as a parent. Doing it all alone was in ways a choice, but Mum seemed only to attract men of such a low calibre. She had a few boyfriends when we were kids, but they were not what we needed as a family. I think as an adult I realised she needed to feel love and loved like the rest of us. They were just there to fulfil Mum's needs, which is why they never lasted. She did not really want the help, she was 'happy' on her own, as she would often tell us.

Mum was a great person for teaching you life lessons. She would often tell me, "I can tell you until I am blue in the face the lessons you will learn from mistakes, but until you make these mistakes on your own, the lessons will never really be learned." Now, I am not saying my Mum decided not to tell us that we were about to make a mistake because she did. She just knew that we would inevitably have to make the mistake, and now was maybe the time for that mistake to be made.

"Mary fixes it," is what we should have nicknamed her, rather than "pishy arse." If Mum did not know how to do something, she taught herself how to do it. She was forever teaching herself things in an age when there was no Internet to google everything, no YouTube videos to watch to show you step by step. She came from the days where you either nailed it or nailed yourself to the wall. You may have been left with your hair upright because you forgot to turn the electricity off at the mains before fixing the broken socket. The days your wallpaper could fall off the wall if you did not know what you were doing. She taught me how to be very observant; if someone else can do it, then why can't you? So, we did it, we did everything, Mum and me. I was always with her doing things, I always was eager to learn. Once when I was a little girl of three, I wanted to help my Mum with the cleaning. We did not have another duster, so I took my knickers off and started dusting the table with those instead, which unknown to me, was making the table dirtier, but I was just trying to help. I was the girl who asked Mum when I would get to wear an Always (period pad brand) like she did, not realising the horror that comes with a period at the time, of course.

Mum really did not understand how great she was in shaping who I am. The older she got, the more she lost confidence in her abilities in what she had achieved. I was my Mum's hero, she told me that often. I often told her, if I am your hero, then you have a lot to be proud of as you made me who I am. I will also admit that the reason I am the way I am, was to avoid being like my Mum in other ways (from a mental health point of view); knowing how to support myself mentally and physically is of great importance to me. Mum taught me that without knowing she did. She showed me through gaining experience that there had to be a better way of getting through everything that happened to me. She would often forget that when she was drunk, she would tell me about her life and her childhood. Then, as an adult, she would want to tell me while sober, and I would say, 'Mum, I know all of this already.'. This would shock her a little. I wasn't meaning I didn't want to hear her story, as I did. I listened to her for hours; it was a growing process for her. She thought I did not have a clue, but her telling me her horrors while I was young gave me an outlook of, is this what I am going to become? Most of my family on my Mum's side have a really bad relationship with alcohol. I did not want that for myself, or for anyone I was around. I do drink, by the way, just rarely and when I do it is not a lot. I can go out and have a few and come home. Most of my family (who if they are reading this will not agree or thank me) cannot do the one drink thing. I realised that depression and alcohol do not mix at a young age thanks to Mum. She did not see how much she was actually bettering me as a person, through her issues. They made me want to be more and want to have better. Being truly fair to my Mum, she was raised in an alcohol-fuelled rage. So, what we got from Mum was better than what she got from her predecessors.

Once Dad left, Mum had to become the great punisher as well as many other things to us. She only gave us beatings as and when we deserved them. She preferred to ground us and use physical punishment less; she would take things from us until we learned. She got to a point with Paul where she had to limit his food to things he wasn't as keen on, as she had already exhausted the options of taking everything away from him. He had only a bed and wardrobe in his room at this point. He was getting bread and butter off of her, as he hated butter. So, I ate them for Paul; this way, Mum would think he had. I loved a "piece and butter" thanks to my Dad. Dad used to wake up at 4 AM, give or take, every single night. He would sneak down the stairs and make "pieces" with jam and lemon curd, as well as taking a load of biscuits to eat. I often woke up with him at that time and he would make me some too.

Mum was a great teacher and leader, even though she was unaware of it. I realise that at points in this book you will think my Mum was horrible, and parts of her absolutely were. However, Mum was mentally ill, as I said before. I will refer to these parts of her as "Mary" because in these moments she was no longer my Mum, and was in a more depressive state than you can begin to imagine.

Mum is the reason I have the career I do and earn a great living. I am a kitchen manager for a well-known company, and I run a team of people. I am better able to do my job because of her. Mum had another nickname, "Mary cloth"; she was a clean freak. The woman got up at 6 AM to do her housework before a ten-hour shift, even though no one was ever coming over to see it. She stripped the beds, took the curtains off, and washed the walls on the same days each week or month, depending on what it was and how often she felt it needed to be cleaned. She never left her bed unmade, not even if she was late. Her dishes were always done straight after dinner. She did not have a thing out of place. It was not her way; she definitely had undiagnosed OCD! However, I now excel at my job and that is thanks to her teaching me the routine, patterns, cleanliness, and level of OCD needed to be a good kitchen manager. To be a great kitchen manager; I say this because people who have worked with me have expressed this to me, not because I just think I am the best. Any manager who has worked with me has said they have not seen a kitchen like mine before, after having seen others in the company. So, I can only share this based on what others have told me. I take pride in what I do, Mum taught me that. She taught me how to do my best in the hopes that it was good enough, so I have now done my best and it would seem it is good enough.

She single-handily taught me things that even people with two parents did not know. Maybe that's because Mum had to go it alone, so that struggle taught her things being in a parenting team would not normally teach you. Being a single mum on benefits must have taught her some serious things too. She did not plan for life to be this way. My Auntie Carol and I found this out when going through her house. Auntie Carol is not a blood relative, but a dear and lifelong friend of my mother's since they were children. She had applied for jobs in London to be on television when she was younger before she had met my Dad. My Mum had big dreams that I knew nothing about. I think after all my Mum had been through, with no one to guide her down the right path to mental stability, she lost sight of all these dreams she once had and all the things she had wanted out of her life. They slipped away as each day in her life passed, especially when kids came along.

Kids bring a sense of selflessness you cannot dream about. A dedication like no other; well, for most parents but not all, but especially for someone like my Mum. She was so dedicated to us, but occasionally expected a little too much from us in return. Mum needed us to be more to her than we could be. This became more obvious to me as I became a teenager and wanted to spend less time with her; that is when her mental health became *very* apparent to me. She needed us to want to be with her all the time. Which was fine when we were kids, and even when Paul was a little older. I would truly consider him as a mamma's boy, whereas I was not really a mummy's girl. In ways I was, but not the same as Paul. As a child I was so shy, I used to hide under my Mum's skirt if you said 'Hello' to me, especially if you were a man. My Mum, like all mums, was my safety net. My hideaway when things got rough, she always had the answers, even if you did not like them or want to hear them. I suppose when Paul was a teenager, and he went out, Mum had me in the house to spend time with her. Once I got to his age, Paul was gone, and when I was out with my friends, Mum was all alone.

I was not a difficult child, especially given what I had been through as a child. I was quiet and did well in school. I was not top of the class or anything, but I was not bottom either. She had an ok ride with me. Recently, when emptying Mum's house of all her things, I read her suicide notes that she had kept from over the years, and they expressed a great sense of abandonment. As if I were purposefully not spending time with her, as if I were leaving to be away from *her*, rather than her realising that I just wanted to be with my friends, like every other teenager. I think because she had always had two kids, now only one around and I was a teenager, she just could not get her head around that I was in fact normal. I was a teenager. A child still, but trying to get out and live my life. I mean, I was also probably trying to get away from her, yes. But so was every other teenager with their parents too. We do not like our parents when we hit a certain age. I especially did not like my Mum when I was a teenager, because Paul died when I was thirteen and the way my Mum changed and the person she became then was awful.

So much responsibility fell on my shoulders, and I had to carry myself and my Mum's feelings and emotions with me every day. Mum always seemed to forget I was a kid. She really expected too much of me and needed me to be her partner most of the time rather than her daughter, which for a thirteen-year-old was not fair. I think she also thought that when I was at school that was enough time away from her, but school is not time to yourself, school is full of fear and anxiety all day long. There are people who are smarter than you, prettier than you, bullies, some teachers who are horrible to you. It was not my place for mental release. I needed time with my friends, away from it all. Mum just could not see it; her mental health would not allow her to acknowledge that I was a *normal* teenage girl, I was not trying to be anything less.

She would tell people who may have noticed how wise I was for a young age, "That poor lassie has been through so much, and then she needs to deal with me on top of that.". She has been saying that to people since I was eleven. I think Mum knew, but in the end, Mary was the one in control of her mind. Mary was a cruel, evil bitch who twisted the very fabric of space and time to make it into whatever she wanted it to be, and then Mum was crushed and buried under her enormous foot. Mum was not breaking free, and when you brought alcohol into the mix, it was multiplied tenfold. Alcohol and depression are a terrible mixture. Alcohol enhances the feelings you already have, so if you are sad you will feel more sad, happy you will be happier, and so on. So, if you are a manic depressant, you will not be full of joy and laughs. You will be full of whatever fun-filled anxieties are in your head that day. Then if you add antidepressants into the mix, you will also have a higher sensitivity to the alcohol you are drinking. Mum could have one vodka (she poured them rather generously) and be pretty much gone with the wind. She was on the highest level of antidepressants there was, and mixing something that tells you not to consume alcohol with it is never a good decision. Trust me, I have seen it first-hand.

I would say from my point of view that Mum was at her worst through my teenage years. I think I feel this way as I was not as equipped to deal with her then, as I am now. Mum was, in fact, at her worst that year because of that mother fucker John (her man friend)! However, as a teenager going through everything that comes with that alone; as well as going through it with my Mum and then having to deal with Mary's outbursts on top of it all was no picnic for me. So, from that sense, I would say that was her worst point.

When Paul died it was honestly unbearable for me. I had so many mixed emotions about it, and rightly so. Paul did a lot of terrible things to me that will follow in the next chapter, so I did not know how I was supposed to feel about it. I'm not sure a single soul could have told me how to feel about it either, and I'm still not sure anyone can. That was a moment of grief that was truly baffling for me to get to grips with. As for Mum, she had spent a lot of years with Paul before she had me, and then it was still a few years before she knew or came to grips with the fact that something was not right with him. To her he was a son, to me he was a dickhead of the highest calibre. She lost her son, her firstborn child; a boy she had raised, and he was now gone from this earth. I have never given birth, but I have been pregnant, and I can tell that giving birth to your first baby would be one of the most precious moments in your life. To then lose a child (that wee baby) would be an awful thing indeed. Mum was very torn about it all; she was always convinced I could not see it from her side, when in fact I could. She never seemed to understand it from mine.

At first, Paul was brought up in conversation all the time; of course he was, we had to plan his funeral. Then time went on, and Paul should have faded away a little. Chats of him should have halted by now. They did not. I asked Mum about it and tried to explain that it felt like Paul was everywhere, even when he was nowhere. The constant chatter about him was getting too much for me, so I decided to pluck up the courage to ask her to maybe just not do it while I was there. Mum had no understanding about this. Mum and my gran would speak of Paul all the time. When he died I just wanted him to be exactly that, dead! Not to come back to life. Paul was never really mentioned before he died, as he was not with us then, so why now all of a sudden was he the talk of the town?

Dying does not make your sins disappear, and to think it does is absolutely naïve and misguided. I cannot express enough that when you have caused someone pain to the magnitude Paul caused me, that does not leave because you are dead. I understand Mum did not know everything Paul had done; in fact, she did not really know much about it at all. I remember Mum once threatened to slap me across the face if I did not tell her what Paul had done to me, this was after he was away from us. I did not tell her because she did not need to know; she was the last person on earth I wanted to go into detail about it with. In fact, this book will probably be the most open I have ever been about it in my whole life. In the end, I got a sore jaw. She slapped the face off me for not telling her what he did. I never understood her need and *want* to know.

When Paul was taken away, I know she blamed me. After all, she was not wrong. It was my fault he was gone, but it was *her* who called the police. I was the exact reason he was no longer in our lives. She became a lot more violent towards me then. Mum had a way of switching that violent streak on and off, especially when she had a drink. As a teenager, I thought she was insane. I thought it was madness; it had to be. How could this be normal? I knew my friends' mums did not act this way. So why did mine? She must be off her rocker. I will not lie, there were definitely times in my life I wished my Mum ill or dead. I didn't truly mean it, but in my head in the moment, I did. Mum was a great mum, but Mary was a self-loathing maniac, who took everything out on me. Being a single parent was such a struggle for her, as it would be for anyone, but especially when you add Paul's behaviours into the mix. Paul was a horrible human being. He pushed my Mum to the limits and then some. Yet she seemed to have this undying love for him. A mother's love, I suppose. Something I guess I don't know much about, except I know if I were a mum, I would have that same undying love and that is why I do not want to be a mum. Well, that is a lie; I do want to be a mum, I want to adopt a child once I have seen the world. When I am thirty-five, give or take, my husband and I will take the plunge and look into beginning our adoption journey. I want to help a child have the best possible life they can. We have already overpopulated this planet; we do not need any new babies; there are plenty in need of a nice home.

After Paul was taken away, Mum's drinking became much more frequent. She would come into my room in the middle of the night, pull my hair, and scream in my face. She would be screaming so close to my face she would be biting my cheek, and she raved on about how I was "an ungrateful wee fucker!", or I was "an arsehole!". I was all the names you can think of and then add some more to your list, then you might then have it covered. I would have to go to school after that, after she kept me up until about 3-4 AM screaming at me, she would come in and wake me for school as if nothing had happened, and go back to her bed while I got dressed for school. I wet the bed twice, once at eleven and once at twelve. I had never wet the bed before, not even as a child. I sometimes would not make it to the potty, but Mum always loved that I never wet the bed. I think this was from fear of everything that had happened to me over the years. I became sick not long after one of those times, and Mum pinned it down to that, but I do not think it had anything to do with that. I think it was from her violence. I pretty much always slept in beside my Mum and one of the nights I wet the bed was in her bed. When I woke up, I was too scared to tell her I did it. I got up and dressed for school and as I was about to leave, she flew out of the room and said, "Did you pish the bed?"

I replied "Yes."

She then continued, "Did you even wash?"

I said "No." I was too scared to wake her up, so I did not wash myself.

She continued, "You are a clatty wee bastard!".

There was Mary, gracing us with her gifted presence. Mary did not have one ounce of kindness in her body. Later that day, I came home to Mum who then asked me what had happened. I explained to her I did not even know I had done it until I woke up. Then I explained I was scared to tell her, and she looked at me as if I had two heads on my shoulders, "Why would you not want to tell me?". Mum used to scream the heads off Paul and I if we did not make it to the toilet to be sick. Once I was helping her put the curtain up and something happened that made me laugh, because it was indeed funny. Mary did not think it was funny at all, she decided to make me stand on the chair with my arms up in the air for fifteen minutes, so I could see how it felt. She stormed off in a bad mood. Mary had a bad temper, she bit things if she was angry at them. If she were building something or putting a cable into the back of the tv and it would not work for her she would bite it and throw it across the room. Not a patient person either. Mary was cruel and could say things that would cut you in two, her heart made of ice. Whereas Mum, Mum had a heart of solid gold that she would give to anyone and everyone if they asked and even if they did not, she gave it anyway. She was a kind, loving soul who would lay herself down in front of a car for you, for no real reason; just if you needed her to do it, she would. People thought the world of my Mum, and she thought the world of them too. Mary was the problem; Mary needed eviction with no notice period. She caused so much grief in our household it was unreal. Mum and I found solace in music in times of trouble and two of our songs were Rose Ave's *Open Door* and Eminem's *Headlights*. The Eminem song really describes Mum and I's relationship down to a T. Mary took over *so* much, and for a long time in my life, Mary was all I could see in my Mum. I think that was linked to her use of alcohol as well as life hitting her hard most of the time.

Our family had the usual politics, so that meant the family never helped my Mum. We were always walking on eggshells with someone or other. You would go to one of my auntie's houses and they would tell you a story, but then say that, "You cannot tell so-and-so I told you that," or "I am not speaking to this one or that one.". It was a rare time when all our family were able to be together in the same room without someone hitting someone else. Auntie Jacquie was something else in our family, and she was constantly causing a scene or a fight. I saw her getting hit more times in my life than I care to admit, as well as my Auntie Lynne.

I'd seen my gran and her fight so many times in my life, it is not right. I witnessed my gran punch more people or get into fights than anyone else I know.

The family drama is not really what this book is about though; this book is about grief. I suppose that caused me grief, so maybe it is a little about that too. One Christmas, I witnessed my Auntie Jacquie being strangled by my other auntie against the fridge in my Gran's kitchen. I am sure she was punched as well. Now, to put things into perspective, my Auntie Jacquie was a massive alcoholic. We did not tell her when we would be at Gran's, because she could not be trusted to turn up sober and not fight with her partner and ruin, well…everything. This year she had shown up on, I think Christmas day. She had come in the door that was always left unlocked, as there were so many of us coming and going all the time. She shouted when she was on her way up the stairs and everyone froze for a moment, knowing it was her but not sure what state she would be in. Aware that no matter what state it was, it wasn't going to be good and she entered the room clearly inebriated. Probably seething, knowing yet again she had not been invited. I know this seems mean, but people tried to get her help, yet she refused it on several occasions.

My Auntie Lynne was there with her new boyfriend at the time, Tony. My Auntie Jacquie sat for a while, ranting and raving about all things old and in the past, then she focused on Auntie Lynne's man. They are twins, you see; Auntie Jacquie was thin due to her alcoholism (I mean wafer-thin), and she asked me to go round the road and grab her one of my miniskirts to wear because she wanted to steal Tony away from Auntie Lynne. She still had it in her to do so, she said. At this point, I believe she got up and started dancing near him and that is when the major cracks started to form in everyone. Patience was wearing thin and finally one of my aunties cracked and went for Jacquie, pinned her to the fridge, and screamed at her. That was the way of my family, they were taught to fight when the going got tough, as that was all they had seen from their own parents, brothers, and sisters. That was what they thought you should do: react with violence.

Mum was a toned-down version of her own parents who thought that by being better than them, even slightly, made what she did right. I suppose in ways it was right to be that way. That is how we begin to make the world a little better and brighter, by trying to delete the badness and replace it with good. I wish Mum could have deleted the alcohol, which I asked her to do so many times.

The older I got, the more I realised the damage all the years of being alone had done to her. All the years of not having a partner; how from a young age I was the adult, and she was the child. I argued so many times with Mum about her alcoholism. I stated on several occasions that it was the one thing that tore her and I apart. She never seemed to be able to link the two, or was just so in denial of it she chose to not want to make such a link. A link like that meant admitting a problem, and my god, she certainly was not going to admit a problem here. After all, there wasn't one. Right?

Certainly, Mary did not let Mum think so. She assumed because she was not like my auntie that she did not have a problem or a dependency, because she did not drink as much as the people you see on the street that you know to be alcoholics. That she herself, you must then conclude, could not be an alcoholic. I do not think my Mum or Mary understood addiction all that well, to be honest. She did not seem to grasp that pretty much anything in your life you feel you *need* to do is an addiction. Addictions are habits you have in your life that are essentially bad. Take eating; eating is an addiction or habit because it is a requirement our body needs to survive. Eating can then become something we use as a tool to make us feel better when we are sad, and there comes the problematic feature of a good habit gone bad. We all have habits and addictions that we take for granted, like the gym. People are addicted to going to the gym, that is a good habit; pile on an eating disorder, and you have a disaster. Mum needed to drink at least once a week. It was once a week no matter what. Mum's drinking distinctly caused her and I the most grief we ever experienced, from her violence being tenfold, to her mood, attitude, her impulsive and erratic behaviours becoming unbearable at times.

As I write this, I question every single, thing I write as I am still in the mindset of protecting my Mum. I cannot help it. I am not trying to paint my Mum in a bad light; she was not a bad person at all, that is why I feel the need for this interjection. I have wanted to write about my life since I was in my teenage years, to help better the lives of others around me, to help people realise that life is tough but that we can all get over it and live a great and happy life if we so choose. I knew that I could not write such a story without hurting my Mum, something I have never wanted to do. She may not have wanted to admit our truths, but I do for the greater good. I know that due to my Mum's mental health it would not be possible to write a book such as this without it having adverse effects on her. I know that even if I would have asked her not to read it, she would have. I knew I would need to wait until she passed away to publish any such thing. I have never put pressure on myself to write it until now. Not long after Mum passed, I knew I had to write something. I knew it would help those around me with any problems they would have in the future, as well as ultimately helping me.

Writing seems to be the one thing in this world that helps me understand and deal with my own feelings. I was up rather late one night unable to sleep, and the title came to me. That is when I got up out of bed, opened the laptop, and started writing away. I thought I would not get the chance to write such a piece until I was much older, as I hoped of course, that Mum would have been with me for at least a good few more years. It was not to be. Mum has sadly passed now, and I will use her death to fuel my fire to write this story for you. To help you understand your pain, to help you know we are all going through things. You are NOT alone in this. Things will get better if you choose that to be your path, if you learn to use what are perceived as weaknesses as strengths.

Happiness is a choice I have learnt. It is a mindset you need to want and adapt to. I feel so many people bask in the glory of misery, much to my astonishment. I mean, I find it in myself too, of course I do, I am human. The brain will make me think about bad things for protection. You need to tell your brain no. Like saying no to that chocolate when you are trying to cut down. You need to tell the brain no; we do not think like this anymore. We are going to spin this to be positive, even during the worst thing you have ever been through, you were taught something from it. What we learn from these things will ultimately help us grow as people. To see it in that light is not easy, but it is a choice. Even when anxieties are filling your head, you can turn them into better things. See it from greener pastures.

Now onto the part I am probably dreading the most.

Chapter 8

The Abuse
(My Biggest Grief)

I realise that for most people, this chapter will probably be the toughest read of your life. I will be descriptive, it will be emotional, heartfelt, real, and most importantly of all, it will be honest. I will explain things in detail that I have not actually told another human being in my life, because it has not been necessary to do so for any reason really.

Can I start with a side note to any younger people reading this? I have walked through my life with more weight than nearly every adult I have known. I have learned that no matter what age you get to, people fear and envy the wise. Just because someone is older than you, does not mean they have lived or gained more experience than you. Wisdom is gained through tough experiences and your ability to get over them. Some people who are older than you will try and make you feel smaller than them. Rise above this; they are not above you solely because their age is greater than yours. If age had anything at all to do with wisdom, then at seventy-five everyone would be Gandhi, but they are not. We can all learn from each other no matter our age. I have helped those much older than me through some of the toughest times in their lives. I am profoundly grateful to have been able to do such things, and it was not because of age; it was because of pain and grief that I was able to do so. Pain is our greatest strength, our greatest sense of being. Pain is what makes us human. The ability to feel the way we as humans feel is what sets us apart from the rest of the animal kingdom. Do not let anyone let you think your experiences do not matter because you are young, because I can tell you right here and now, they do. Use your experiences as your key motivator to be better than them, to do good things with your life and help people. We all make mistakes in life and we should try not to judge others, but we are only human and sometimes we do. You will make major mistakes along your path, be terribly sorry for them, and move on using them as your way to being a better person. Let us move on to the nitty-gritty.

As I stated earlier, it seemed to have started when I was two. However, I do not really have any recollection of this, it was just a story my Mum told me. For me, the memories of it started when I was maybe four or five. I was abused by my brother until I was nine years old, physically and sexually. I was a victim of sexual abuse and I'm now a survivor of it. A proud survivor.

When I was a little girl, I lost my innocence very quickly and very young. This loss was driven by many reasons that I have already begun to mention, but this was the principal reason. Paul was most definitely sick, he had mental issues like no other. I do believe Paul must also have been abused at some point in his life. He was not just born the way he was; people rarely are. He was damaged while young by someone, someone close to us and who knows what they had done. Unbeknown to a few people in this family, Paul mentioned a few names while he was in the young offender's institute. Whether they are true or not is another thing. He did say he was in fact abused; however, he never sought to bring them to justice himself. They are still out there and part of this family. Unfortunately, if Paul chooses not to pursue like he did, there is nothing that can be done by anyone else out there.

Paul, I believe, started showing concerning signs quickly. I do not know the first thing that triggered my Mum to suspect him, I just know she was very suspicious for a long, long time. She used to sit on the stairs at night in Daldowie St. to see if she could catch anything occurring in the act. Having had a bad upbringing herself, she had a "spidey-sense," one of the many senses a human being develops as part of our own defence mechanism when we have experienced a lot of trauma, pain, or hurt. This happens to be one of the most accurate senses one can develop; Mum proved that to herself and to those who doubted her. Professionals doubted my Mum, so did friends and family too at first. I know myself that I have an ability to see through anyone to help defend myself from being hurt by anyone ever again. It is kind of like a superpower, to be honest, and I always astound people with it. I am very rarely wrong about a person; I am also rarely unable to read who someone is. You become so good at being able to read facial expressions, body language, and speech patterns that putting them all together helps you develop a sense of who they are very quickly. I suggest for those of you who do not know what I speak of to buy a book on body language and study up; it can tell you so many things about another human being. Mum would be sitting at the top of the stairs trying to listen to see if she could hear anything that she could catch in the act. She never did at this point.

Paul would sneak into my room in the middle of the night and abuse me when Mum was asleep, or if he knew she was still going to be up for a while and she would not catch him. It is odd for me to type things in a way that will help you understand it from my child-like mind. I am no longer a child, but I am very much able to take myself back to those moments in a second. I was only around four when I had my first memory of being abused by Paul. A four-year-old mind is so very easy to manipulate to do things you want them to do for you. I know, because I was that four-year-old. When I was four, Paul was nine. A nine-year-old boy vs a four-year-old girl. He was smarter, better schooled, and more powerful; what chance did I have? He told me things like he would hurt Mum if I told anyone at all what he was doing. He threatened to hurt me, as if he were not already. He told me he would make Mum go away, that if I told, our family would be more broken than it already was, given that my Dad had already left at this point. He was also able to tell me little things, meaningless things. He would threaten to tell Mum the smaller things I had done, like stealing a biscuit out of the cupboard without asking for it. It was easier for him, as I was so young, I didn't know his threats were not monumentous.

I am to this day still terrified of the dark, something I do not think I will ever get over in life due to so many horrible things happening to me then. However, it happened in the daylight too. Yet I am not scared of the day, although I am riddled with anxiety so maybe that is my day terror. Paul was what we referred to as "fly", he knew how to get about from day to day without being detected. Not always, of course, but most of the time. He seemed to think it was all a sort of game. He would think more people would want to join the abuse game; he had built it up in his head as something that was all ok.

Eventually for me, I gave into Paul for a few years because I did not know what else to do, and you start to think of it as a kind of normal. This must be what happens to everyone, right? Wrong! My Mum used to beg and plead with me to tell her if someone had touched my flower; I have such a distinct memory of it. She was in the bath and I was standing by the side of the bath. I was very young, as I remember the bath seeming so big to me. She lay there and said, "Anneliese, you can tell me anything like that, no one should ever touch your flower. That's yours, and if anyone ever does and you don't think it is right, you tell mummy right away, ok?". I was silent for a while and I replied to her, "Mummy if I told you, you would hate me forever."

Now, as an adult, I look back and think, "You fool, why did not you tell her! You should have told her right there and then." But how was I to know Paul was not going to take my Mum away from me. I could not possibly know at four he did not really have the capabilities to make her go away, although I suppose people at nine have killed so then again, maybe he could have. Sometimes I fought Paul, and sometimes I did not.

There was a show recently that depicted a rape scene called *Thirteen Reasons Why*. A lot of people complained that that scene was not accurate, and I can tell you right now it was accurate. In fact, more people act that way than don't. If you research it or have experienced it, you will see that it is not like the movies depict, giving in means it is over quicker, means they get less from it too. Remember that any time you sit having a conversation judging someone for not fighting back. People who go out to rape you get a thrill from the fight. I am not saying simply give in or give up, but sometimes that is all you can do. In fact, sometimes you, the person, is simply gone for your own protection. You become numb to a state of mind, not just body, a trance-like effect comes over you and that is your way of protecting yourself. For some, it is fighting them. Fight or flight applies to rape too, only the flight is you going off into your mind, time to tune out and let your eyes glaze over. The thing is, if you are raped you do not have a choice in this matter, if you are abused on occasion you do. Sometimes you cannot disappear into your own head and you will fight them. I fought at these times. Paul would often go off and return with a knife or something else threatening, especially as I got older.

I have a memory from when I was young, we were at my gran's and apparently, Paul took a notion for abuse. I used to have this cassette player, double-sided, long and thin, and it had an ability to play tapes and record tapes as well as a built-in radio, all very modern for its time. I had taken that with me to my gran's to listen to my music while we were there. We had been told to go in the room and play; this was my gran's bedroom. Paul had some sort of wrestling tape with him, and he decided to record over it with the sound of him abusing me, while my family were all sitting in the other room. The worst part of this was he brought that tape out one day, and of course I knew which one it was, you do not forget something like that. He brought it out to let my Mum hear a song on it. I panicked! Was he, who threatened me to never ever tell my Mum anything, about to literally play a tape of him abusing me to my own Mum? He knew I was panicking; he could see it in my eyes and he loved it. He loved to watch people suffer; I was sure he had forgotten he had done that to the tape. Maybe he had brought that one in by accident. But he knew, he knew he had then taped over it with the wrestling music again. He knew it was not on the tape. He did it to torment me. To make me feel so embarrassed, scared, and humiliated with no remorse in his face or eyes. In fact, he made sure to look directly into my eyes at the exact moment I knew it would be coming on and smiled at me as the song just kept on playing. What a bastard!

Paul used to make drawings, too. They were sick and horrible, and no one can know how many he had made and how long he had been making them for, but his imagination was wild. He would draw (not very well) things about what he would do to a person, or what he wanted to do I should say. These drawings all included me and Mum, and pretty much any woman Paul knew. It would include details of them doing things to each other as well. Again, including me and Mum in that. I have no idea where a boy like that got these ideas at such a young age, an age where the Internet was not even there yet. Paul was cruel to animals too; he never ever liked them. And, as they say, that is the very first sign.

I also have a memory of a night, again in Daldowie St., where Paul had a friend stay over and they both used me as an instrument for their own pleasure. As I say, Paul thought it was all a game. He wanted to get as many people to play his game as he could. I was older now, maybe seven by this point. I cannot actually imagine what this friend of Paul's must have been thinking at the time. After it though, this friend of his told people about it and they were shouting "Slimer touches his sister" outside our house (Slimer being Paul's nickname). Can you imagine being seven-year-old me and having to hear that, as well as getting abused by this "friend" of Paul's who had absolutely no objections to it at the time? Yet he had the audacity to tell people about it. I understand he was young, I do, but it does not hurt me any less!

That night was awful for me. I was passed back and forth from one of them to the other like I was an inanimate object. I can still remember the feeling of them pulling my pants off me, and it makes me cringe every time. While writing this, my face is red with embarrassment. To only be later humiliated by it because Paul, although good at threatening me, was not actually good at thinking about what his actions (getting his chum involved) would cause later on. He was not smart that way. He was a master manipulator, but not good at looking at the bigger picture of what any of his actions would cause. After this night, my Mum clearly heard these people shout that, and her suspicions were in a way confirmed. But she couldn't do anything about it without any evidence or an eyewitness account from herself or me. I was not talking!

GRIEF

I was always shy, quiet, and hidden from men when I was young; can you blame me? Men to me were awful things that seemed to only cause me pain. My Dad left, pain. My brother abused me, pain! The two closest men in my life hurt me, one way more than the other. Men just were not my thing. The reason I was so quiet though, was because Paul made me be quiet about so many things. I had to hide my life away from everyone for fear of losing my Mum, or anything or anyone else he would threaten me with. I was a shy wee girl who remained quiet my whole life really. Until now, of course.

I slept in my Mum's bed a lot to avoid being abused, and no matter what night it was, if I was in my own bed, I always woke up knowing something had happened. My pants would be on wrong, pulled down hanging halfway down my legs, my nightdress way up around my neck. There were always signs or hints something had happened whether I remembered it or not. My abuse from Paul started with him rubbing my flower, to putting fingers in, to finally full-blown rape or penetration, whichever you prefer to call it, and all things in between. I am sure you can paint a good picture without me having to go into mass amounts of details. As I stated before, Paul's imagination had no limitations. Paul used to say things to me like he could not wait for my pubes to grow in and my wee boobs to appear. He was disgusting. He did not care whether it was a boy or a girl, he was happy with both. He had a longing for threesomes in his drawings; he wanted to be penetrated himself too. He was very unwell, a boy at eight or nine should not know about or have any of these thoughts.

Paul had a girlfriend when he was thirteen or fourteen and was still choosing to abuse me at the same time. I assume with her being young herself, she wasn't willing to go as far as Paul would have likely been pushing her to at the time. I even wonder if he ever tried to *recruit* her to the abuse game! Paul was always trying to maximise the players and she certainly met his criteria. He would most likely have wanted her to be a part of this game, letting her in on all his secrets, and hoping she would want to get involved. I can't help but think of her from time to time. It makes me wonder if he ever tried to push her to further their sexual encounters, did he abuse her too? Did she know I was abused? It can be funny how the mind thinks of these things from time to time.

I do not have many detailed memories now that I am older; I was the numb girl most of the time. To this day, I regret not telling the police the entire story of what he had done, but my Mum was with me pretty much the whole time I was being interviewed, so I didn't want to go into detail. Plus, telling what seemed like one million strangers just wasn't my thing at ten. Mum finally caught Paul. She was convinced for a while Paul was trying to kill her, and I think she was right. She used to ask me to smell her tea, as he was putting bleach in it. In Paul's warped mind and imagination, she was dragging his plans into the ground. My Mum finally caught Paul in the act one morning in our living room when we lived in Dundyvan Rd. Paul had clearly decided he was wanting to live out one of his fantasies. I think Mum must have been awake and heard him, or possibly me asking him to stop. Our hallway was long and creaky, so it was ridiculously hard to sneak up it. She was obviously determined to do so and catch him in the act. She did!

Finally, I thought I was going to get free of it. Boy, was I wrong. I also felt so humiliated that Mum had caught him and seen me that way. Now, I know that Mum had seen all of me before, she ran my baths for me, but when she saw me like that, I knew she would be feeling shame and so was I. I am not sure I have ever felt shame quite like it. Now, I had nothing to be ashamed of, you might be thinking, or I at least hope you are because you are right! I do not to this day have anything to be ashamed of at all. I was the victim, and am now the survivor of sexual abuse and one sexual assault. Paul's 'friend' counts as a sexual assault to me. I see abuse to be something long-lasting and sexual assault as a one-time thing. At least that is how I segregate it. I haven't mentioned Paul's friend to many people over the years. He was a little older than Paul at the time, fifteen maybe. I do not feel a need to name this person, nor do I feel the need to pursue anything now. There is no point. That is all in the past, put to bed, and I am here to tell the tale. Mum had seen me with my knickers pulled down by Paul, Paul pinning me to the ground, about to abuse me. She walked in just in time. Can you imagine that at all in your mind? Maybe you can, and maybe you do not want to. Understandable. I wish I was not able to imagine it, with the detail I can.

That day, a lot of things changed. Not for the better though, like we had thought they were going to. This is where I passionately believe that people who get into counselling with absolutely no real-life experiences just shouldn't be allowed. I am sorry if you are sitting there as a counsellor, having been through nothing much in life, but once you read this maybe you will understand my point of view.

I am not exactly sure who my Mum spoke to or where she went for help on this matter, but we were referred to family counselling. Honestly, one of the worst experiences of my life. We were given a counsellor named Elswith Jenkings, a horrible woman in my eyes who later leaked information about me and my family that she should not have. She became the person we went to see on a weekly basis as a family unit. It was in the Alexander Hospital, up next to Blairhill station in Coatbridge. It was no longer a hospital, and we were in a small newer-looking unit at the very back of the building. We would go there and wait for ages to go in and see Elswith. She was not a kind woman, and for someone who had kids of her own she did not seem to understand them at all, or how to speak to them. She certainly had no idea how to get me to talk to anyone.

We were all forced to be in this big room together with the two-way window, which I knew people were behind. As someone who had been abused, I like to see the face of those judging me and my situation; I could tell one of them was a man. The room had huge windows, making it easier to see through the two-way glass. I could at one point see there were three figures in that mirrored window. So, I was not saying a thing. In fact, I hid behind a chair and barely answered any question this woman asked me. She spoke to us with a sense of snobbery, which I am almost sure she had. To someone of her stature, we were nothing. A piece of crap on her shoe, eating away at the taxpayer's money. Why should she want to fix us? It was very clear very quickly she didn't want that.

I appreciate with Paul still being rather young and myself being so young, they did not want to just rip the family apart and lock Paul away. It is rehabilitation first, then we move on from there. After a few sessions, Mum had shown her Paul's very descriptive drawings that included Elswith herself as well as Mum and me in these images, to show her what was going on. They asked Paul to explain why he was making these pictures. Why he thought that was right. Could he explain them to her? They would ask me what Paul was doing to me, while Paul was still in this room with us! I mean, I surely do not have to explain; that is absolutely appalling behaviour to ask me in front of my abuser, what he is doing to me! I was about seven or eight at this point. What did they think I was going to say to them? I know Paul got his own sessions as well as the family ones. However, I did not get any special ones. Unfortunately for Mum, the more I did not talk, the harder it was for her to prove her case, even though she had walked in on it herself.

They went through Mum for her abuse of alcohol and blamed her for Paul being able to abuse me. Which honestly was not fair to Mum. He would do it no matter where we were, no matter the time of day or night, several times in a day, even when we were playing outside. I am not saying if Mum had a drink it didn't make it easier for him, because of course it did, but it did not matter either way. He would get his way if he wanted to. Elswith told Mum she was a liar, and that she would leave Paul with her own kids, that she trusted him. Unfortunately, a degree does not give you a "spidey-sense". You can study your whole life and never understand what I am talking about. Fifteen degrees will not enable you to know what it was like to be me and understand what it was like to be in my shoes.

That was clear with Elswith and all the nice faceless people behind that glass. Going about my life, wondering if one of those people had seen me on the street and recognised me because I was abused, haunted to a level I am not sure I am able to depict to you. It is just not something you want anyone to know about you without your knowledge. Elswith did have one session with me in my house. She was there to see Paul, I was in the house at the time and she asked my Mum if she could see me on her own. Mum had said yes, she showed me this weird and strange book. It had this page that is now burned into my memory for life. The page was full of cartoon drawings of men who were naked from the waist down. An image I would rather be rid of, but unfortunately, I am not. I have no idea what it was she thought she could do for me by showing me such a book, and I recall her asking me to point at one for some reason or other. I must tell you that all of this only added to my pain and suffering. The industry might want to consult a person who has been through similar things before they decide to put books like that in front of another abused child. Not even just the book. The people behind the glass, the way the questions are worded. Not even trying to get to know us before asking an amazing number of embarrassing questions. I know these people have a job to do, but there is a way in which these things can and should be conducted, and that was not it.

I recall not long after this going to the Moira Anderson Foundation and meeting a lady called Sandra Brown; it is her foundation. She was amazing and her foundation helped me so much. I think I may have gone there after Paul was taken away, actually. I remember it helping Mum and I. She had books for me to read that did NOT have pages with men and willies all over them. I recall her saying something to me so well, as Mum and I used to repeat it all the time, that "Paul is a liar and a fibber; he can't be trusted. You have done nothing wrong, and you are not to ever feel ashamed in your life for the things that happened to you." - She was so right, and hit the nail on the head. I can highly recommend her foundation to you. If you are an adult who has suffered abuse, you know someone who has been abused, or a mother or father who has a child in my situation, please give foundations like this a try. They are so helpful and full of professionals as well as survivors who can help you along the way. Look them up, get help, or donate to the cause; they will be so grateful to you for it.

Abuse is such a hard thing to deal with, and the grieving process for this is long and hard and at times so trying for a person. All they want to do is disappear. I had friends in school who I told I was being abused, and I feel bad forever telling them because as an adult, I realise that there is a weight that is carried from being told information like that. I wanted to get rid of some of that weight as it was a lot to carry back then. Having been so young and naïve I did not think about what that information would do to the "wee" people I told it to. Do they still think about that from time to time? Is it something that they blocked out? Is it something that haunts them?

If I told you my story while we were kids together, please accept my apology and know that I was just struggling to cope and wanted to tell someone. I *needed* to tell someone about it. Someone who was not a grown-up. I think I maybe hoped I would come across someone who it was also happening to, someone who would understand. I did not, which is not a bad thing; I am in ways glad I didn't, nor am I even sure I really wanted to. I think I wanted to feel a sense of being normal. In a world as big as this, I am still not the norm, that is a good thing! No one I have ever told my story to has been through anything like what I have been through, especially not with the chapter that follows. I have often in my life felt so alone in it all. I have met people with worse stories, but not similar. Never like mine. Never anyone who could directly relate to it. Maybe one day I will. I am sure if you read this and were touched by it, you might want to reach out to me. I wish I knew how to open my own foundation like Sandra Brown did. I wish I could spend my day helping people with my story and guiding them on to a better path. Showing people that you can succeed no matter what you have been through. That what you have been through is the biggest strength you have. It is your most precious asset. Not a shame or burden but a glimmer of hope to those around you, a beacon of light to those wandering a dark and narrow path. You can and will be whatever you want to be, no matter what you have been through in life. The world is changing, and people want to feel empowered, so go out and empower them!

Chapter 9

The Light

I do not recall the exact date the next event took place. I was eight or nine, and that would have made it the year 1999. Mum and I had been in the living room watching TV. Mum had two vodkas with Irn Bru. She and I were having fun and laughing, while Paul was in his room playing with his PlayStation.

We had won that PlayStation; it is the only reason we had one. Mum had entered a competition on Nickelodeon while I was out playing and Paul was in his room. You had to answer a question to win. They called back and of course asked to speak to her son or daughter, whichever had entered the competition. Mum flew into Paul's room and said, "Quick, Nickelodeon are on the phone, we have won a PlayStation."

Of course, Paul thought she was taking the piss out of him. He said, "Aye, aye, mum, I'm not that stupid."

My Mum screamed at him, "Fucking move, Paul! They are on the phone right now, we have won!" He got up and went into the living room and she was right, they were on the phone and we *had* won. A spot of good luck; she kept it for our Christmas that year, which we were obviously thrilled about. We never thought we would have a PlayStation, so to be getting one no matter the way, was enchanting to us.

Back to the night in question. Mum and I were in the living room, and suddenly, a few pieces of paper slid under the door. I remember thinking, what on earth is this all about? While Mum was reading them, I knew something was wrong. She let me see it, and as I looked, she said "What did I do wrong?" She then paced for a while, not knowing exactly what course of action to take. On the paper, there were so many detailed drawings of Paul's deepest fantasies, featuring people from our family including Mum and me. It was clear he had an extensive imagination, but it was horrific viewing them. He had written side notes to make sure his points were clear; you certainly knew what his expectations were. Paul was the one who received the counselling and got 'help'. Here was my Mum having been told she was mad, that Paul was normal, and my Mum was imagining things. Yet here we were months later and he was worse than ever. Mum explained to Paul on many occasions that he would be placed on a sex offender's list, she pleaded with him because he would be taken away from us and he would never be allowed to come back. She also told him that if he ever met someone one day and wanted to have children, they would be taken away from him. She was unbelievably detailed with him about the outcome of his actions, and he still explicitly defied my Mum's rigorous advice. Paul's bad deeds did not simply stop at sexual thoughts, he was also a thief who would steal from people if they visited us. He was a liar with no remorse, a guilt-free human with a long trail of damage left behind him.

Mum finally cracked. She was beyond trying now and decided to take the last and most drastic measure she thought she could. She called the police. The police saved me from a life of more abuse and torture from Paul. I do not recall the length of time they had taken to arrive. I do not even recall the waiting process, except my feelings of fear and enlightenment. I had a glint of hope in my eyes and in my heart because *finally*, I was about to be free of my abuser. This filled me with a fear of the unknown; I wasn't sure how I was supposed to be feeling at this moment in time. Should I have been sad about any of it? I mean, he was still my brother after all. Was it ok for me to feel so gleeful about the whole thing? What must my Mum have been thinking or going through at that time? I know she would have been torn in two. As a mother, she is supposed to be able to protect us both, but now she had to make a choice that would only protect one of us. Her son, her firstborn, was being taken away.

When the police arrived, I recall feeling a sense of terror. My fear had amplified because it was not just thoughts now, it was fact. This was happening, and it could not have been more incomprehensible. Those feelings were evident. I did not know exactly what was going to come of this, only that something was coming. I knew it would have consequences for me, both good and bad. The two officers, one male and one female, came in and spoke to Mum and me first. Mum had made Paul aware that the police had been called, and she locked the front door so he could not run. I have no idea if he thought she was kidding, but he continued to play on his PlayStation. When they arrived, he knew it was serious. Mum and I had spoken to the police about everything that had happened, Paul's individual counselling and the family counselling that had taken place. Mum explained to the police that despite showing these people (who were supposed to be mental health professionals) Paul's drawings, she had been told that she was mad and that she was the problem. They had asked Mum if she had been drinking, and if so, what amount had she consumed. They then did a thorough check to make sure she was of sound mind while answering questions about the situation.

I told them what Paul had done to me, but they did not need many details before the male officer asked where Paul was. He decided to cuff Paul and put him in the back of the police car before coming back up to speak to Mum and I. He asked if he could look around Paul's room. I recall my Mum panicking as we had pirated games for the PlayStation in there and she was concerned they would fine her or arrest her for it. The police were with us for a few hours, taking statements and explaining to Mum what would happen next. They explained to her they would be in touch about Paul's whereabouts, as she was still his mother and legal guardian. I remember thinking these two police officers had not dealt with a situation quite like this one before. It was in their eyes as they looked upon me with astonishment as I explained very briefly with minimal details what Paul had done.

I did not realise how little I had told the police that night until a few years ago when I decided I was going to make a start on my book. I had always wanted to write a book about my abuse, but I was never sure where to start. I decided to investigate, and wanted to track down my court case first. I sent a few emails and was redirected to a few different places before finally reaching the correct department. It was in Edinburgh, not far from the castle. They have all the old case files and court transcripts in there for safekeeping and appeals, amongst other things. It was that day I realised I had not told them or the courts even half of what Paul had done to me. I was obviously so scared and ashamed of it; I did not want to tell anyone about it. At that age, I don't even think I would have had the vocabulary to clearly depict what I had been through.

Later that evening Mum was awaiting the phone call to tell her where Paul would be kept overnight. I believe he was kept in the cells for his first night, then transferred to St. John's young offenders institute where he would remain for the duration of his detainment. He was there until he was sentenced, which was almost a year after the day he was taken. At that time, I was still in primary school; only ten years old. It was not easy to go through life with your brother having disappeared from the face of the earth. Mum came up with a surprisingly good lie to cover up the fact he was gone; she would tell people he was away to live with my Dad down south. There were very few people who still maintained contact with my Dad at the time, so who was really going to question it? The problem was some people would question it, terribly rude people. However, Mum only decided to tell people her cover story when they asked her about Paul or mentioned they had not seen him in a while. Mum should have spread the story openly to allow the seed to be planted; by not doing so, she was creating suspicion and causing more people to question her. They seemed to be relentless in asking her questions about what was clearly a private matter. People have no shame at times and have a selfish need to know information, despite knowing that it might bring pain or embarrassment to the other person/people involved.

When Paul was gone, it was so liberating for Mum and me. There was still a lot of stress to come from the courts and lawyers, but all round I was able to be a little girl again. A ten-year-old as she should be, free from fear of the night, and fear of what was going to happen. The fear was not always gone, of course. It was always ultimately there. It began to dissipate, and it was better knowing in my heart that it could not happen to me again. I still woke up at night with fear, sometimes waiting for the darkness to descend upon me, but it would never come again. I was finally able to be alone in my room. I could go to sleep in there, it was now a safe space for me. I did not need to sleep in with my Mum for protection. I must have spent most of my young life sleeping beside my Mum, to save me from a worse fate.

I don't think she minded me being in her bed; we enjoyed a wee cuddle up with a Disney movie and then sleep. I would put my head on Mum's belly while she stroked my hair, which to this day makes me fall asleep almost immediately. I can imagine sometimes I must have come to be a burden to Mum. I remember some nights she would encourage me to go into my own bed and sleep. Maybe she needed a little privacy, or craved the bed to herself, or maybe she knew it wasn't healthy for a girl of my age to still be sleeping in beside her mummy. Whatever the reason, she was right to try it. I think her main suspicions aroused from me consistently wanting to sleep in beside her. I think I wanted to be with her as I also had abandonment issues because of my Dad leaving. As I previously stated, I was distraught when my auntie tried to take Mum away for a night out. Once Mum had been gone for a while, I was able to settle down and have a lovely evening with my gran and grandad. Gran would often buy me an ice-cream cone from the ice-cream van so she wouldn't have to feel bad about having got one for herself.

Unfortunately, that freeing feeling came to a halt not too long after Paul was taken away.

Chapter 10

Court

I remember this god-awful process very well. Before I had any time to digest the horrors that had befallen me, I was already having to relive them. Perfect strangers were coming into my home with note pads and writing down every word I said about what were the worst moments of my life. After the police had taken Paul away, I never dealt with them again. From there it was the Procurator Fiscal; her name was Laura. If our justice system is unknown to you, let me quickly explain. When the police come across a case, they pass the case on to the procurator fiscal for them to deem it worthy or unworthy of court. The seriousness of the crime will determine whether you go to the Sheriff's Court (your local courthouse) or the High Court. Our case was deemed serious enough for the High Court in Glasgow.

I remember Laura being one of the first to sit with me and go over what had happened. I then had to go over it with her staff in a lot more detail; these people were trained to deal with kids who had suffered abuse. My Mum, who was deeply religious at this time, had asked our priest to come and sit with me while I spoke to them. I obviously did not want my Mum to have to hear what went on with Paul and me. Anyone who came into the house to question me had to press me for the information that I *willingly* gave up. I just wanted for it all to be over and done with, and I had hoped that now Paul had been taken away it would have just evaporated, disappeared, poof… no longer any need to talk about that ever again. Yet here I was in a room with a priest and people I had never met in my life, and would never see again, having to tell them everything that had happened to me in the dark.

In the end, I didn't give up much of the information they required, only the bare minimum. They made me point to parts of myself he had touched or had done things to. All they ever found out was that he had touched me in places and inserted fingers; that is all I was willing to give them. All they had to go on was my initial statement to the police. I can recall them trying to express how safe I was and how it was ok to tell them more; no matter what it was, I was going to be ok. They did everything they could to try and get me to tell them more; they could tell I had much more to give, but I just couldn't do it. I was too young, I wasn't ready. It didn't matter how serious it was, they could keep telling me it was ok on a loop, and I still wouldn't have told them anything. I wish to this day I was able to expose the full truth to them. I did not understand by law they were not allowed to tell my Mum a single thing I had said. In fact, now I think of it, Mum was not allowed to be with me while I spoke to *all* those people to make sure she could not influence anything I was saying. It had to come from me. That is why only the priest or a teacher would have been allowed to sit in with me to help me feel at ease; unfortunately, they did not help.

I was having to lay bare things I had not disclosed to a soul. Not really, not fully, not properly, not like this! I recall Father Dempsey saying to my Mum that he could feel me looking around trying to catch his eye, but he sank himself into the chair to avoid my gaze, as he did not want to feel like he was influencing things I said. I was just looking to make sure I was safe; I needed his eye contact to reassure me I was safe in that room with those people, and that I was doing ok. That it would *all* be ok. I absolutely understand his point of view, though. I cannot imagine it being an easy thing to do, to have to sit there and listen to things like that from children. I personally hope he has only ever had to do it on this one occasion. The man who came to speak to me from Paul's lawyers was lovely and kind. He showed me how to draw a swan without lifting the pen off the paper, something I can no longer remember how to do, but he had a way with kids. He got me to open up to him very easily by showing me one trick, as well as telling me about his kids; that made me feel at ease.

Ironically, I told him more than I told my own lawyers, even though this in no way benefited me but I was unaware of this. I was *alone* with this man! He had a much better strategy to help me through showing him the parts of my body that had been defiled. It did not seem to feel as bad to tell him the things I needed to, so I was glad to have him, plus he was the last of the people I had to talk to about it.

After I had told both sides of the parties my story, they left me alone for a long time, or at least at my age it felt like a long time. I had to be examined by a police doctor, that was fun! I went with my Mum that day to our doctor's surgery, which was Coatbank medical practice in Coatbridge. I always went to the left when we entered this building, but today, we went to the right. I did not really understand this. Mum and I had been assured it would be a woman who performed my examination. We sat in the waiting room, Mum seemed calm and was doing her absolute best to reassure me, unfortunately for her it was to no avail. I was shaken to my core about this.

I remember sitting there thinking, "Do they all know why I am here?" or "They can tell, they are looking at me funny." I always thought at times I had a sign on me that said **victim**! People knew I was tainted and did not want to be near me. That could not have been further from the truth, but you cannot help but feel that way. It is something you cannot shake; Mum even referred to this sign as I got older, hoping she would have someone who could relate to these feelings. Her hope was worthwhile as she did, I knew how she felt. People describe it as a dirt you just cannot wash off, and to me that was evident. And boy, did I shower! I scrubbed and scrubbed, yet it never seemed to leave me!

It had stained deep into my skin like a black hair dye, or red wine on a white carpet. The real reason for this stain was in fact society. Society gave me that stain from fear of what others thought of such things. I was abused; was that my fault? Absolutely not! I was the victim; was that my fault? No, it was not. Did I, as a three or four-year-old, ask for it? No, I did not! If you have ever dared to insinuate a single person has asked for it, you yourself are broken in the mind the same way Paul was, and I would highly recommend seeking help before it grows in your mind and infects all of your other thoughts. I watched footage of a Trump rally recently, where a man interviewed Trump supporters to their own humiliation and told them facts that none of them clearly understood. There was one man in particular at this rally, and I will quote him directly. He said, "One man's sexual assault is another man's flirtation.". Therefore, society makes you feel ashamed and powerless. What an insane thing to say. Trump has set us back years, especially for kids like me. People cannot see the damage he does to those of us who have suffered in this life. Allowing men to think that they can "grab her by the pussy" and it will be all right.

My name was called out by the nurse, "Anneliese Gallacher," my heart sank in my chest, I let my Mum go in front of me. As she walked into the room I turned and ran away screaming at the top of my lungs, crying. I had never been this way in the doctors before, and I did not know how to get out. I went through a set of double doors and turned to my left to another set that I thought we had come through to get in. I was met by a locked door with a keypad entrance. As I turned to run the other way, my Mum caught a hold of me. She was humiliated, rightly so. I cannot imagine what people around us must have been thinking at the time. When I say I was screaming, I mean screaming hard; I am not sure I have ever wanted to escape something so much in my life. Then I remember having to take my trousers and pants down, the nurse sitting me up on the bed and asking me to lie back, touching my feet together and letting my legs fall open at the knees. Then suddenly, a man walked in. I shot up from the table, ready to bolt again. This time, Mum had a better hold of me. She and the nurse helped calm me down and explained that the lady doctor was not available at this time and that is why it had to be a man who would do the examination. I was not ok with it, but what else could I do? It needed to be done.

I remember them talking me through the steps. I got a long cotton swab inserted into me first, then a few other instruments. There was damage, but the way the doctor described it was, the polo mint was still intact, which was the part that technically makes you a virgin. He could see I was inflamed and even given that Paul had been gone a while now, he was able to determine I was in fact abused. I was inflamed on the inside, but at least there was no permanent damage done to me; I was ok. The polo mint I refer to is the part that makes a woman bleed upon first losing her virginity. Not everyone bleeds, but they will usually snap, mine had just been stretched. He said by the time I would lose my virginity properly it would have repaired itself. I remember thinking that my Mum was ok with my outburst as she was amazing sitting there next to me making sure I was ok the entire time. I had done a similar performance when I was getting an injection once, my BCG for the second time around. She did not speak to me much on the way home that day. I think she did not want to be mad at me, but she was. I cannot imagine it was easy for her to have had to sit there and watch me going through it all. I am sure if in those moments she could have taken my place, she would have. She could not, though, and I think a part of her hated herself for that. She battled with herself daily about knowing whether she had done the right thing by me, as she could see it was bringing me pain. Knowing if she had not, it could have led to an even worse fate. Mum was unable to hold on to the feeling of knowing she made the right choice.

After all these things were said and done, the court dates started to come in. I say dates, as there were several. There were other family members present as witnesses. I assume they had to give all their statements the same way I did. We were called into the high court so many times to then be sent home the same day as Paul kept changing his plea. This holds up the full process *every* time. I was taken out of school for this process each time we had to go at ten years old. I remember being taken back to school on one of the days because there were still about two hours left until the end of the day. People were fascinated by the fact I had shown up at a random time. I tried to explain to a few of them that I was in court; of course, none of them believed me. Why would they? They had no reason to think I was not lying through my teeth, fabricating it all in my mind. I really was at court, though; I was the star witness to unspeakable crimes committed on me by those I was supposed to be able to trust in this world. A big brother to most is a blessing. He was supposed to pave a path for me in my schools, show what we were made of and capable of, fight off any bullies I had, or any boys who tried anything. Instead, I got abused by one of the people who was supposed to protect me in this life.

Then he did not have the courage to make a decision on whether to take credit for what he had done, or to pretend that none of it happened.

There came a day though when he did not change his plea, and we were set to go in. I was offered a few methods of how I was to give my evidence. I could be in a room where I would be on a tv in the courtroom, unable to see anyone or anything, not knowing who was asking the questions, or when they would be fired at me. Or, I could go into the courtroom and have a partition placed around Paul, so I did not need to see him. I went for the latter, not a huge fan of a faceless audience as previously discussed. I wanted to see who was asking me these questions; as you recall, I told you about my "spidey-sense" that works for me in all settings. I would be able to see the character of these people right through their god-awful questions. The courts decided not to wear their wigs that day, only their robes, so I wouldn't be scared.

We were in a small room, not too far from the courtroom, waiting to be called. Naturally, I was up first as I had the most evidence to give; I was the key witness here. There was a man who escorted me to and from the courtroom. I am unsure of his title or purpose, but he was there for *me*. He may have been a counsellor as he was allowed to sit behind me, and if I got upset, he would take me for a break. He was a lovely man with a kind face. The official clerk was more intimidating. He was so tall with black hair with these big black eyebrows and a stern expression, yet he was also kind. I assume someone like him must carry so much weight from living a life in a courtroom. These people do not get enough credit for the work they do, the volume of horrendous cases they must endure and the families they must deal with. I was taken in and sat in the podium/witness stand. Due to my age, we had what was called a closed courtroom. In typical criminal cases, anyone can walk into the high court on any given day, go into a courtroom, and watch the cases as they take place. Any member of the public can do so by law unless the circumstances of the case do not allow it, which was the case in our trial.

I took my seat. I did not feel nervous for now; I had told so many people my horrors already at this point. I felt numb, similar to the way I used to feel in some of my moments while being abused, I was in a state of shock. I have heard many people claim that when they are in shock, they don't know what they are doing. However, I have been in what would have been called shock many times in my short life. I must tell you they are some of my most clear and vivid memories I will ever have until the day I die.

I sat in this podium, which seemed exceptionally large to this ten- or maybe even eleven-year-old now, as this case had dragged on for quite some time. It was over a year before we finally got into court for real. I looked up from it; there was a huge round table in front of me, the scary-looking man was sat behind me to the right. A full jury was looking at me, trying not to stare, but they could not help it. I think it was my age that threw them off. Having been on a jury now myself, I realise that sitting there in the jury seat is one of the scariest experiences in one's life, the power to decide whether a person is innocent or guilty is enough to haunt you for a lifetime. At the round table, there were a lot of people, too. I remember thinking, 'What do they all do? Why do they need so much paperwork?'.

There was a lady in front of where I knew the judge was going to sit, and another person in front of her who was dictating the case and recording it on tapes too. All records are still kept to this day in Edinburgh, six floors underground in a government building. I knew where Paul was, or at least where I thought he was, as there was a partition that seemed a little out of place in the room. They announced the judge entering. I was scared now. He was a lovely human indeed. He helped ease me into it by asking what I had got for Christmas that year, as the case was in either January or February of 2012. He made sure I fully understood that if I needed a break, I just had to make him aware, they would let me take as many breaks as I needed. He explained how the process would go and what to expect. He did not mislead me with anything he said. He assured me it was ok to be upset, and I was in a safe zone.

They explained that while I was giving my evidence I would not be allowed to go back to my family at any point. This was to ensure my family were not able to interfere or sway my thoughts. If I were to take a break, I could not see my Mum. I have never been one to dilly dally in times like this. I might want to avoid it altogether for as long as I can, but once I know I must do it, it is best for me to keep on going until the end. Get it over and done with, so my anxieties don't have time to build up in my mind. I have had anxiety for a long time. I was unaware I had anxiety as a child, but I have had it since I was a young girl. Based on my life events, I am not surprised; it makes sense that one would come away with some sort of lasting effect. Call it a disease or what you will, the label does not really matter, your ability to understand it and overcome it as best you can, does.

I sat there and Laura (the procurator fiscal) went first, as with all cases. She asked me a series of questions which I answered honestly and openly to the best of my ability, despite Paul trying to distract me with his consistent cough. He was not sick; let me assure you of that. He was hoping to instil fear into me by every now and again doing just one individual loud cough, so I knew he was *there*. It may have been his lawyer's strategy to get him to do this, as it could have caused me enough distress to make me fumble in my ability to give my evidence. Unfortunately for him, I was not about to clam up, nor was I scared either. I knew I was nailing him here; I knew this was my opportunity

GRIEF

to nail him down. I was in control now, not him; I had the power in my hands. His lawyer was a complete bitch to me. I am aware of her job role, but you can ask questions in a way that you are not a bitch to a ten-year-old and still get your point across. She did not take that approach; she was in full swing bitch mode. She gave me a drawing of a vagina, and asked me to point to what hole was the right hole for sex! Just because I was abused did not mean I would know where the correct hole was, as if that proved a god damn thing. It was to her surprise that I was smart enough to work out in my head it was the middle one. However, it was pretty much a guess using common sense, thinking in that moment about where my pee and poo came out, and then where all the bad things happened.

After her being a cruel, insensitive bitch to me, her final thing, the last thing she had in the bag to help her to win this case, blew up in her face. She lost because I was not an incompetent eleven-year-old! Unlucky for her. If cases have been lost for something so silly and stupid, then we need to rethink our full justice system. I personally feel they should not be allowed to show images like that to a child in a courtroom. I feel the use of that image was damaging to me. I had not received my talk about periods at school yet; I hadn't even had my first period. She took more of my innocence in a setting that had already taken parts of my childhood from me. I remember Laura having something to say about it. Not long after that Paul coughed again. This upset me a little this time, and the lovely man took me out of the room to get a sip of juice. He told me to wait while he went and got some juice from my Mum. Mum immediately asked the man how I was doing. Was I ok? Did I need her? The man told a white lie to Mum, explaining I just needed a drink and that I was doing great, nothing to worry about. I am glad he said that to her; it is what she needed to hear.

I went back in and gave the last of my evidence. The judge thanked me for everything, saying I was brave and I was well-mannered. Thanked me for my time there and for helping them in their case. Wished me good health, and let me leave. Then I was able to see my Mum again. I was not allowed to tell her anything at that point though. I believe Mum was supposed to go next, only she never had to. Paul had heard enough and decided to plead guilty. I do not know if his lawyer had advised him to, or my evidence shook him, and then he realised that what was in his head was just that, in his head and his head alone! The nice man came and got my Mum in a rush and asked if she wanted to be present for his sentencing. She said she did, and was rushed away. It felt like she was gone such a long time, and she came back a little different; I think it had finally all sunk in for her.

Paul was sentenced to six years in a young offender's institute. He was to be moved from his current one, where he had been for over a year, and taken to St Mary's. As far as I could tell, he was not happy about this. I do remember that Mum and Gran visited him from time to time. Mum would come home angry because Paul was getting a better life in there than me out here. He had a swimming pool, PlayStation One, loads of games for it, able to buy new clothes, football grounds, an allowance he was able to build up to buy himself things if he was well behaved and much more than Mum and I had on the outside. I think she could not understand it from them. He was supposed to be thinking about what he had done and being rehabilitated, not shown the time of his life where he was able to do things that I on the outside could not. I always hated when Mum visited him with Gran, as I knew I would have to hear about him for some time after. I know that he was my Mum's son, I appreciate that. However, I was also her daughter, and the last thing I wanted to hear about was Paul. Mum never told Gran the real reason he was in there, or if she did, not the full extent of it.

Mum did not understand that speaking of how great he was caused me more harm. I always wished Mum could have tried not to talk about him in front of me. At New Year's at my gran's, it would always end up just me, Mum, Gran, and Grandad. They would both end up in tears about Paul and the fact he was not there, and I just felt like saying, "Hello! I am sitting right here!". I did express this to Mum one night when she had a few drinks in her. At first, she was very understanding, we spoke it through and she was sorry for it. But as the night drew on and she had a few more drinks, she brought it back up, and now I was a bad guy, and that was not my intent. I see it from Mum's side; all I asked her to do was try her best to see it from mine.

I know he was her son; I was so *aware* of that. I was still the same kid who told her if I confessed to her what was going on, she would hate me for ever. I was the kid who had kept my mouth shut for years from fear of breaking up our family even further. I just did not want to hear how Paul was this saint, which he really was not. He stole from everyone, including my Gran at times. If you went out of the room and you left your purse, Paul was in it. If there was a lot of change in it, he helped himself, assuming you would not notice because he did not understand or care to understand the value of money. He thought because we never had any money that if your purse was full of money, you must have been so much better off than us. This is where he was not correct; people did notice at times and Mum would be the one having to take the storm for it, paying them back with money we did not have.

A while after Paul had been sentenced, Laura had come by the house to speak to Mum. I assumed it was a prearranged meeting, but I do not remember Mum telling me about it. It would seem I was entitled to compensation for what had happened to me. Mum received this on my behalf, as I was too young. The forms were awful to fill out as you had to tick boxes about what happened to you. The weird thing was, it told you the amount you would be rewarded for the different things that happened to you. Mum and I were shocked by this and wondered how many people must have lied on it. We did not lie, we only put what we thought was right and that had happened to me specifically. I was awarded around eleven thousand pounds for what happened to me.

Reflecting on it now, that money should be held for the victims who are too young to receive it until they are old enough to deal with that money on their own. I don't think Mum should have had it, although she did do the right things with it. Mum paid off all our debts, and there were many. She took us on our first-ever holiday abroad; this was, unfortunately, her only one which makes me so sad while I write this. We went to Gran Canaria. What a time we had while we were there. I got into a nightclub and danced with my Mum and the tour guide, as well as all the other people who were on the same holiday as us. We had such an amazing time. I got Mum to come into the water in the pool up to her waist. Mum was so scared of water that if it got over her ankle, she would start to have a mild panic attack. I got her in though, even got her to let go of the edge of the pool and walk towards me. This was astounding for Mum; she was so scared, but she did it! Then she never came back in the pool again, but she did do it. We bought clothes for going on holiday too. We bought a new JVC 32", which at the time was a very top end TV, one of those silver ones that came attached to a stand and had a super woofer and surround sound with it.

We also bought this amazing HiFi, also by JVC. It had everything; a turntable, three-foot speakers, double tape player, karaoke, radio, a six-cd changer, and so many more features. It got so much use in our house, the neighbours must have hated Mum, but she would say 'fuck them' as she turned the dial up a little more. She had headphones with it, which for me was one of the worst things. She would forget she had them on, but would still attempt to sing The Jam at the top of her lungs while I was in bed trying to sleep. Mum also tried to sound like Paul Weller, and let me assure you, cats were howling at the moon when Mum let soul escape her body with these dreadful headphones on. We also got new TVs for our bedrooms as well as video and DVD players each. It's safe to say that although I am wildly grateful for all that money and what it did for Mum and me, it really did not help with the grief of the situation. It did not for one-second ease my pain or suffering. It did not allow me to suffer any less, live in any less fear, or take away that dirty feeling from my skin. It was just money to me; it did not change what had happened or take us back in time to make it stop. No, it was just some paper that allowed that Mum and I to live a little better off for a truly short while.

Chapter 11

The Hang Man

In what must have been August of 2003, Mum received news that Paul would get out on early release for good behaviour. He was due to be released in January 2004, meaning Paul was gone from us for about four years now. This meant a lot of upheaval for Mum and me. We had to move to a new house before Paul was released, as he wasn't allowed to know our address. A restraining order was placed upon him for my benefit, that would last his or my whole life, whichever came first. Mum was straight onto the council and was able to get emergency housing. We moved three streets away, as if somehow that would have stopped him from finding us. I understand Mum not wanting to move too far, but we moved from Whifflet … to Whifflet! We could have at least moved to another part of Coatbridge. The bus I got to school drove right past the old house. If he had wanted to find me, he most certainly could have. It would have been so easy for him to just follow me one day, or for me to see him on the street. Restraining orders only work if you can call and report the person on time. I had very mixed feelings about the whole thing; I was scared about it all. I could feel the fear from my Mum; she was scared too. What could she really have done if he did show up? What was she prepared to do? She had already called the police on him once; would she have to do it a second or a third time. If she did have to, what did that mean for Paul? What did it all mean for me? As a mother, my Mum was pushed to her limits. Limits very few people in this world will really understand. I hope minimal people ever have to go through what she has been through.

After the move, I think it was all explained to Paul in a lot of detail that he could never come near me again, or Mum for that matter. He was never again in his life allowed to be with his family. He would need to go back out into society and deal with it all on his own. His eighteenth birthday rolled around on the first of October. Mum and Gran had decided not to send him anything for his birthday that year, as they felt if they did, it might give Paul the wrong impression. He may have had the false idea that everything would return to normal after he was released. Paul had a girlfriend in that place too; her name was Gail, she was in there for something herself, I imagine. I think it had all been too much for Paul to handle.

On the 28th of October 2003, I woke up for school. It was a good day. I had a great day while I was in school, and please believe me when I say great. It was one of the best school days I had ever had in my life. I floated through that day as if a weight had been lifted off of my shoulders; unbeknown to me, it actually had been lifted. This was one of the days I would usually go to my Auntie Lynne's and Uncle Tony's for my dinner after school.

I went to St. Patrick's High School, all thanks to my Auntie Lynne, in fact. When I was deciding what school to go to, I had a choice of Columba High, a school my full family had attended. That included

Mum and all her siblings, as well as all my cousins, and Paul. I didn't really want to go to a school that would ever associate me with Paul for so many reasons, or to be associated with someone called "Slimer." Imagine hearing, "There goes Slimer's wee sister." Sister to the boy who disappeared, and no one knew why. The questions I would get, the taunts I would get, for just being associated with him, not a single soul understanding the damage they would be doing to my mental health. I had been put down for Columba; I chose that school because the majority of my friends were going there. Only three pupils from my class were going to St. Patrick's High.

I feared new things; after all, I did have anxiety. One day Auntie Lynne was in the bath. I was sitting talking to her while she was in there, on the toilet but not using it, just sitting there keeping her company while she was in. She could see I was troubled and asked me what was wrong. I poured my heart out to her about not wanting to go to Columba, wishing I could go to St Pat's instead. She said, "You need to tell your mum, sweetheart." I explained I had caused enough bother already; I had told Mum that I wanted to go to Columba already, so Columba it was going to be. Auntie Lynne decided to tell Mum what I had entrusted to her out of worry and fear for me. I was annoyed at the time, of course; I was eleven. But I have never been more pleased that I felt betrayed in my life. St Pat's and its staff really shaped who I am as a person today. They had such an amazing force of staff who were able to create exceptional bonds with me, even teachers I did not have for any class know me now. I think that is an amazing thing. It is also a rare thing too. To have the vast number of staff able to build up a trust in you, because they all had this trust in each other.

They stole things from each other's departments and held them hostage, writing ransom notes back and forth about how to get said item back. One of them was a sheep from the geography department; these men and woman really loved their environment, and it really showed in the way they taught. Of course, not all of them were incredible, but 90% of them changed and shaped people including me. I could not be more grateful to them for showing me this act of kindness, as I can imagine some of those people had absolutely no idea what I was going through or had been through. They just tried to keep me smiling. One thing every teacher had in common as I got older in primary and secondary was telling my Mum I lacked confidence. That is where my anxiety took its hold over me. I had the brains but, in an exam, I could not get over my nerves. Still to this day, I am the same. It really is not fair as I know the answers, but cannot find them under those sorts of conditions. I cannot do anything about this system; however, at times I wish I could for the younger generation around me.

My school day had ended, and I walked down the hill with my friend Marianne. We said 'see you tomorrow' to each other; we had laughed together all day that day. I went on into the gates of the flat where Auntie Lynne lived. They lived in Coats Flats at the top of Coatbridge Main St. As I walked in the back gates where the car park was, I looked up to Auntie Lynne's house. Sometimes Mum and Auntie Lynne would give me a wave as I came in the gate, but today there were four faces at that window staring at me! This was highly unusual and very odd, as they didn't stop looking at me even after I waved, I'm not even sure anyone waved back at me. I recall getting into the lift and pressing seven. As I walked out, I turned right as I always did; there was a red door with a glass panel on either side of it that took you to the three houses on that side of the floor. I could see out of the corner of my eye that my Mum was standing at the door, waiting for me to arrive. This was most certainly odd behaviour from her. I always just walked in on my own.

Anneliese McDaid

I opened the big red door and noticed her face; she had clearly been crying. I knew something was wrong! I already felt it from the moment I walked in that big red gate. I asked, "Mum, what's wrong?"

She said, "Nothing hen; come in. I need to tell you something." I explained I was bursting for a pee and it could not wait for anything at all. While I pulled down my pants ready to pee Mum was standing with me, not an unusual thing in my family.

I said sternly, "Mum what's wrong? Tell me now!"

She said, "Anneliese, Paul is dead!" Well, my god! I was not expecting that. Of all the things my anxiety had allowed my mind to think, this was not on the list. It hadn't made the cut, hadn't even been in the process of making the cut either. The flow of the pee that I had so desperately needed for a few hours now stopped dead mid-flow. Just halted itself. Shock, I guess, at its finest. Mum broke down. I got angry at first, said to Mum I wasn't going to the funeral. I didn't want to go.

I felt as if he got to escape and yet, here I was, drowning in the pain he had already left me with, and now hitting me with all this pain and confusion. How was I even supposed to feel? My brother had just died, yes. How was I supposed to feel about this, though? Was he ever a brother to me really? Had he ever been? Should I be sad? I was sad, but should I have been? A question I kept asking myself. We went into Auntie Lynne's living room after that where I remember feeling like there were a lot of people in there. Mum had told me she had spoken to my school and that annoyed me for the most ridiculous reasons; when a person dies, you do feel a sense of entitlement to know before other's do. Why? Who knows, really? I have seen it in people so many times. Paul was the only person I truly felt it with, though. Mum had told random people before she told me. I was so annoyed by that, and to this day I am not sure why. Maybe I wasn't annoyed about that at all, maybe it was the grief giving me something to be angry about. Something to focus my anger on. It is so much easier to deal with feelings if you can rationalise them, and I was able to rationalise my anger and point it at my Mum. Was it right? No. I had only turned thirteen on the ninth of October myself, so I didn't know any better. I didn't know then that is what I was trying to do. Paul leaving made Mum and I closer, but Paul dying was another thing entirely for us.

When he died, we weren't allowed an open coffin. I was convinced for a while that he wasn't actually dead, that they had set it all up so I would think he was dead. I imagined them giving him a new identity and moving him away so he could live a normal life. I used to say this to Mum all the time. Even now at thirty, I wonder about it; it's a good theory and it holds up. This is clearly madness, but the fear I had of him still being out there somewhere was so apparent in my grief of him dying. I was so sure he wasn't in that coffin; I wrestled with Mum over this, I wanted to open it and see if he was in there. I asked her several times to get them to open it to make sure he was in there. I just needed to know that we were actually putting this asshole in the ground once and for all. I know now in my mind it was him and he is gone; the fear of him not being gone, however, was overwhelming.

She didn't know what I was going through, and I didn't know what she was going through at this point. She had never been abused and then had her abuser kill himself. I had never had a son who abused my daughter and then killed himself. The police had been looking for Mum in the early hours of the 28th; they were sent straight out to find her. Of course, we had just moved to a new house, so they landed on the doorstep of 404g Dundyvan Rd at 4 AM. They woke some poor unsuspecting soul out of their bed only to find out that soul was not my Mum. They took a while to get hold of our new address, as they had to wait on the housing office opening. The police had still arrived early, after I left for school at about 8 AM before my gran was due to come round and meet my Mum at about 9.30 AM that day.

Mum described every element of it to me. She had the police chap at the door; you can never mistake a police chap. They asked Mum, "Are you, Mary Gallacher?"

She replied "Yes."

They went on to ask if she had a son called Patrick Gallacher, and Mum, confused, said no, she did not. The police corrected, "Sorry, Paul Patrick Gallacher." Mum said her heart sank at that moment, not because she thought he was dead, but because she thought he had done something wrong, maybe worse than what he had done to me. Tried to escape maybe? Her mind wondered as they asked her if they could come in. She let them into the house, and they asked her to sit down. Mum wasn't a sitter when she was worried, more of a wanderer. She sat as they asked, and they explained that Paul had hung himself in the middle of the night between rounds of the guard checking in on their rooms. He had hung himself on the back of his toilet door. It wasn't until we received Paul's things and his three housecoats, all with no belts in them, that we realised he must have tied them all together to do it. He left a note that read:

> *To Whom it may concern,*
> *look, all I want to say is thanks for all your help*
> *but I've been through too much in too short a time, and all*
> *I can ask, for who get's this first, is tell my mum and*
> *little sister I'm just so fucking sorry, and tell Gail*
> *I'm sorry and this is my way of killing the pain once and for all.*
> *Paul Patrick Gallacher*
> *P.S. Tell Will and John they've been such good mates and I'm sorry.*

There was also a picture photocopied onto the paper; I assume it was Gail. It was written on what looked like the page of a school notepad; we got a copy, of course. So, I don't know how the photo of this girl was actually attached to the page itself. Not that it matters anyway; just something I think about sometimes. Mum called my gran to come round immediately, then her day consisted of telling our family, her sisters and brother, and going to the school to inform them in case I needed to be off for a while. I went to school the next day. I will never forget it. Marianne and I would sometimes walk to school, so I would walk backwards to get her and meet her on the hill on the school's street. When I met her that day, she barely got to say hello before I blurted out that Paul had died and that he had hung himself. She said immediately, "You should not be at school."

I didn't want to be surrounded by people who were sad he was dead, because I wasn't sad, I was angry at him and glad in so many ways. He freed me too. I was free to walk this world never having to worry about walking into him or explaining to someone that I have a brother, but he can't come within a certain number of feet near me. I was so angry at him though; I knew Mum wouldn't take this news well, and here I was *again* having to pick up the pieces because of him. Why couldn't he have just been my normal big fucking brother? Not a perverted weirdo. Why? Why did so many other kids get it so normally, and yet there I was at thirteen, abused and scared? I had to convict him in court, scared. Brake up my family, scared. My Dad was gone, scared. Paul had caused us all so much pain and torture, but he had no idea (or maybe he did, I thought at times, one last punishment for Anneliese) of the hell-storm he brought down on me from this whole thing.

I had to convince my Mum to tell my Dad, partly for selfish reasons of wanting to see him again of course, and also because I knew he deserved to know. He was, in fact, his son too. Mum told Dad, and Dad came to the funeral, he apparently had to ask which one I was out of myself and Marianne. Now, Marianne and I look nothing alike. Never have and never will. I have long dark hair with sallow skin and I look like my Mum and my Dad, I have their features too. Marianne was very fair, she burned easily in the sun and had freckles; she also looked nothing like either of my parents. I remember being so mad that he had to ask that, however, I also realise that he had not seen me since I was four or five, so I had changed a lot. He was also nervous, I imagine, and his son was dead from hanging himself.

Paul's death was briefly reported on the news that day. They weren't allowed to use his name as he had only just turned eighteen. I think they gave a special allowance that it might hurt me too if people could link me to Paul; that would be all the more painful for myself and my Mum. I remember my Mum sitting and watching it, as someone had told her it was on the news, so we watched it over and over to see if we could find it.

Paul dying was a whirlwind of emotions and pain, and a tremendously rough time for Mum too.

Chapter 12

Mum's First, Second, Third Attempts

It was again in October, my most favourite and most dreaded month of the year, and after Paul died something broke in my Mum. I think it was just one thing too many for her to hold on to, with everything else she had been holding onto in her own head. The keywords here being 'holding on to'. Not too long after Paul died, Mum was falling apart. She was worse than I had ever experienced her yet, her violence and her drinking had increased fivefold, her attitude had changed exponentially. She was no longer my Mum, she was Mary.

Mary had been in her a long time, but now Mary was taking her over who she was. She had seen the doctor, received counselling, had a CPN (community practice nurse), she even had a psychologist at this point. Mum was a mastermind at making these people think she was ok. Any time she ever had them, which was several times in her life, she found a way into tricking them all, including the doctor too, into believing she was fine. It's easy to do; I mean, they can't really argue because if you are telling them the right things, they aren't allowed to call you a liar. That is not their job. They are there to help those who *want* help, but unfortunately, some people do not want to be helped, not because they intentionally refuse it, but it's all they have ever known and new is scary, so they avoid new.

How do you live without anxiety if it is all you have ever known? How do you live without fear and worry if it's all you have ever experienced? Someone lifting your pain from you is not an easy thing for a person to accept. I appreciate not everyone will understand what I am banging on about here. When all you know is pain and suffering, it really is difficult to wake up and say no to it all. I want better than this for myself. The fear of failing and somehow feeling worse than you do already is one of the scariest things to ever face. I know, it was me once. Mum always thought I didn't understand her goings-on because at such a young age I had made a choice to let it all go. I decided to say, "No! I am not living like this anymore, no more will I remain a victim. It is time for me now to walk across the wire and take my place as a survivor." Mum didn't understand that, but that did not mean I didn't understand her want and need not to let go.

If I can teach anyone a single thing from my experiences, it is to let it all go and let it all go fast. The longer you hang on, the harder it gets to let go. Having watched my Mum battle with her demons for years and years, clinging on to every single thing that had ever hurt her, holding them all tight; the older she got, the less she was able to see a way out of it all. Imagine it all as strings in her hands, only they were not in order. The more strings you added to her hand, the tighter she had to hold, so she started to wrap them around her hand so they couldn't get away from her. Her hand started to become strangled. Losing that all-essential circulation to a part of her that needed to move and breath all on its own, but she couldn't breathe, and there was no movement so she was stuck; trapped in a web she had made. It was so tangled she couldn't claw her way out of it. That's often how Mum felt at times.

When you have experienced so much trauma as Mum and I have, even when you let it all go, when the next thing comes along that tiredness that comes with stress comes back tenfold. It's as if your sleep debt all catches up with you at once and you become too mentally, physically, and emotionally exhausted so fast, so hard, and so deep again; it is as if it never left you. Mum had that on top of the fact she hadn't let anything go that caused her this tiredness. The tiredness is completely manageable if you get up and keep routines as much as you can. Use meditation and breathing exercises to help you through it all. Eat right and get the body moving as much as you can so when you do sleep, the quality of that sleep is at an all-time high. You *can* help yourself; it *is* in you to do it. So, do it.

It was the day after my sixteenth birthday. Mum had let me have a party that year in the house while she was at work, and knew she would get in around 8:30 PM to oversee the goings on. My boyfriend at the time, Marco, was there as well as a few other friends I had. It was a great night; Mum had a few vodkas near the end of it before everyone went home. This was the day that Mum had started. By this point, I had been awakened several times on many other occasions with Mum saying she was going to kill herself. In the middle of the night, my phone would sound, and I would have several messages from Mary telling me I was worthless, a waste of space, a shit daughter, an absolute horrible human being; you name it, and if it was bad or horrible it was indeed me apparently. I would say it was the vodka she was drinking that she should have redirected the anger towards. This was rather common, especially since Paul had died. Often, I would get a mix of messages while I was trying to sleep for school, or her barging into my room to hit me or scream at me, or whatever took her fancy that night. All three on occasion; that would depend on the drink or how much had been consumed. I had walked into her sitting with all the pills in front of her several times, telling me she was going to take them all and that no one could stop her. At the age of fourteen and fifteen, I had no clue what to do. I was already a book that was slammed shut. I wasn't going to be able to openly chat to someone about these things. I had tried to be open about my court case with people, and they thought I was mad. Why would this time be any different? So, I didn't tell anyone. Mum wasn't only texting me though; at times she would send her goodbye messages to a few people.

Luckily for me, she had sent a message to a few different people on the night in question. She had been texting me abusive messages all night, a goodbye message, and so on. I finally got to sleep for school, and when I woke up I thought to myself, "There she goes again; another fake suicide attempt." If I had acted upon all of them, I would have been looked upon like the boy who cried wolf. I will never forget any time I tried to tell an adult what Mum was like, they just dismissed it; she was my mother and I had to respect that! Except I wasn't trying to disrespect it, I was asking for help, maybe without the right words yes, but I was asking for help with her. She was a lot to carry while I was still trying to carry all my own baggage and deal with everything that had happened to me through the years. I had no help and no real role models; except Sharon, who I will mention later. I had no one to confide in that had experiences like mine.

I had woken up that day for school with messages. I didn't read them, as I didn't need to feel any worse than I already did about myself just before school. I went into the kitchen where Mum had left all the pill boxes lying on top of the work surface, clearly placed there for me to see. I thought she was just at it again, trying to make me feel bad or trying to make me run in trying to save her. I went off to school thinking nothing of it, although I was a little worried as I always got when Mum did this. Thoughts went through my head like what if she was dead? What if she was dead and I had done nothing? How was I even to know if she was going to mean it this time or not? She had always said I would be better off without her; what if she was right? Was I about to find out? Did I want to find out? No, I did not want to find out what life would have been like without her. I went on through my day.

I believe I had mentioned it to my friend Marianne, as she was used to Mum's dramatics. I wasn't afraid to tell her about Mum in any way. Marianne had often lived through it if she was staying over at my house. She would see for herself how Mum could be, messaging me all night or coming in to scream at me, and so on. As the school day went on, my Auntie Annemarie tried to call me, but I didn't answer, as I was in school of course. It did worry me, but she was all the way in Aberdeen so how worrying could it really be? I left it again as she tried to call persistently. I went to my graphics class and she had text me by this point, asking me to pick up, saying that I needed to pick up. I asked my teacher, Mr. Gibson if I could take the call. When I finally answered, Auntie Annemarie explained her deep and growing concern because Mum wasn't picking up the house phone or her mobile. Auntie Annemarie is not family, but a lifelong dear friend of my mother, and also my godmother. She said she would call the police for me, but asked me to head over to check on her and let her know what I found. Now, for the life of me, I can't recall if my Auntie Annemarie spoke to my teacher or what happened. I think he got someone to go and get Marianne from her class. He seemed to know why I was leaving, so it would make sense if Auntie Annemarie spoke to him.

I was so scared as I explained to Marianne why we were going to my house. She called her mum or dad. We got to the house quickly, it was only five minutes from the school at the time as the schools were merging together. I was in Columba High for three months until the new St. Andrew's High opened. I remember putting my key in the door. There was silence as I opened the door, and Marianne asked if I wanted her to come with me into Mum's room. I refused and said, "No, you can wait in the living room." It wasn't her scene to see, depending on what state Mum was in. I opened the bedroom door and immediately saw how Mum was really struggling to breathe. I could see her body seemed to be trying to leap up slowly as she was trying to inhale. I left the room having no clue what to do.

Auntie Annemarie called me back for an update on how she was. I explained, and she said, "We need to call 999, hen, do you want me to do it?" I agreed with her. I didn't know the first thing about calling 999. She called them, and the paramedics showed up. As they took Mum out of her room, she threw me this look as if I was *nothing* to her, a look of disgust. I will never forget that look, as it had such an impact on me. I went to Marianne's to wait on my Auntie Annemarie to arrive. They were driving from Aberdeen and she was on the road as soon as she could be. That night I stayed in my own house and had asked Marco to come and stay with me, as I didn't want to be alone. He was amazing and in shock about it too. I will always be thankful to him for showing me such kindness and understanding that night. It was awful, Mum was so apologetic; it took me a long time to forgive her for that and she said she promised she would never ever do that to me again. That promise came up and was used against me several times in my life, as if somehow I was the one chaining her here on earth, where she didn't want to be.

She broke that promise on several occasions. The next year I was with my boyfriend Martin. He had stayed at our house for the night. I came out of the room to go in and check on Mum as we had both been receiving abusive texts all night, and after the last time, I didn't take chances. As I walked to her bedroom door, I could see a bathrobe belt hanging over it! I was alarmed to say the least. Was I going to be able to open this door? Was my Mum hanging from the back of it? What if she had fallen off of the door and I wasn't able to get in to get her? As I pushed the door it was light. I remember a sigh of relief coming out of my mouth. She was sitting in her bed. I very rarely swore in front of my Mum; even at thirty, she taught me to respect my elders, so I do. I swore at my Mary that morning.

I was so angry at her as she thought the whole thing was funny. She had fallen off the door and hurt her back! All a big laugh? I was so engulfed in anger. It was one thing to put me through that, but to bring Martin into it was another thing entirely. He would have been traumatised if she had been dead. She had also messaged my Auntie Annemarie telling her she had tried to do it the same way Paul had, joking about it as if it was normal. This was my Mum on all her meds and getting the help she needed from all the right people. Mary hated Martin because he took me away from her. I realised as I got much older that my Mum had more abandonment issues than I had ever thought possible. No one had left my Mum. I found it strange. She was terrified of losing me and at the same time tried her best to push me away as much as possible. If she were a box of chocolate, I would have named them confusions. I still hadn't forgiven her at this point for the first time she had tried to end her life. She once told me of a time she had taken pills but vomited them all up. This must have been a second *real* attempt that I was unaware of at the time.

Several times after this, I would go in to find her in the living room, drunk, with all the pills all over the floor telling me she wanted to end it all. I have walked my Mum back from the edge more times than any soul should have to do for anyone. She was always determined to die. I would be better off without her; that was her go-to phrase! I always hated that side of her. She was a psychotic horrible being, full of resentment and anger. I was always to blame for everything, though. Mary had an inability to take responsibility for her own actions, or her role as a parent at times, too. Whenever I pleaded with her about how I was a teenage girl, and she was supposed to be there for me, I was a fool who simply didn't understand. I was a parent to Mary, and she was my child. That was our relationship the minute the police told my Mum Paul was dead. She was so scared of me dying that she allowed me no freedom. What she didn't realise is the more she tried to smother me, the more I wanted away. The more she caused me pain and hurt, the further I would run from her, in my mind. At least Paul set me up with the ability to split into two, a trick I used for much of what I had to suffer with Mary. I loved my Mum! Mary? I HATED her!

Chapter 13

Out in the cold

I can readily understand why anyone reading this story might be thinking I am blowing my own trumpet when I say I was a good kid, but I was a good kid. I did well in school, passed my exams despite all of what was happening with Mum and Paul. I wasn't a down and out, I was a 100% attender. I didn't stay out past the time I was allowed out, and I followed the rules 90% of the time. I wasn't sleeping around with people; I wasn't into drugs and I didn't really drink unless Mum allowed me to at home with her or if she allowed me and my friends to. She called and asked their parents first, of course. I wasn't a bad kid, and I didn't deserve to be kicked out of my house at sixteen. I am aware this is the legal age one can get one's own house. However, I had no desire to ever get my own home at this point. I had been with Martin for almost a year at the time. He was seventeen and we went to school together. He added me on Facebook, commented on my photo, and from then on I fell for him. He was kind and a gentleman. Unfortunately for him, he chose me! My, was he in for a wake-up call. It is fair to say Martin did not have the same background at me by any means. He had a working family; they were much richer than us. Being older now, I realise they weren't really rich; they were working class. Much better off than us, of course. My Mum had only got her first job when I was three in Asda Coatbridge. We had nothing, and most looked upon as if we were nothing.

I will always remember this night until the day I die; it was an awful memory. Mary had decided to come along and play for a while. She was a few vodkas deep when I got home from Martin's mum and dad's house that night. To put it frankly, she was pissed! I went into the living room, where I was immediately attacked by her words. She then made me stand there while she hurled abuse at me for quite some time before telling me to leave. As I was walking out, she blindsided me and pushed me into the door. By doing so, I smacked my head on the door frame. I fell down, got straight back up, and continued to my room where I shut the door, and laid down in bed with my head thumping, crying and praying for a peaceful night ahead. Maybe she was done and would leave me alone now.

Nope!

She came bursting in at around 2am. She started screaming in my face that I was a little cunt and she hated me, and I didn't love her. Her teeth were scraping off my face the full time she was doing it. Somewhere inside I snapped! I drew my legs back and pushed them as hard as I could into her to get her away from me. I instantly flew up out of the bed like a woman possessed. I grabbed her by the hair and screamed in her face, "I DO FUCKING LOVE YOU! WHY CAN'T YOU SEE THAT, YOU IDIOT!"

Of course, all Mary heard was the word idiot. "Oh, so I'm an idiot now." she carried on with more and more. I couldn't take it anymore. I started taking my pjs off and got into my clothes, pulled joggers on while she belted me in the back with both her fists clenched. I didn't care; I didn't even feel it to be honest, my adrenaline was too high. I put a zipper on with nothing on under it, and I was ready to leave. Mary grabbed my arm tight and she dug her nails in so hard that she had blood dripping down my arm. She didn't know that but I could feel it and saw it after I left. I begged and pleaded with her to let me go. She would not. I asked her again to please let me go. She said, "If you leave, you are never ever coming back here." She dug in harder. I had no options left; I wasn't staying there any longer. I couldn't stay any longer. She had taken enough of me and my own mental health, and I couldn't cope with it anymore. I was done. I grabbed her other arm and bit her as hard as I could until she let me go. When she did, I ran for the door, down the stairs, and off I went. She screamed at me from the door as I walked down the street. I was an absolute target for anyone that night. I was so lucky I didn't see any untoward characters on my travels that evening. I called Martin, sobbing and apologising. I didn't know who else to call. I knew my gran wouldn't help me, as this was proven later. Gran was old school. It had to have been my fault, it couldn't have been my Mum, as she was the mother after all. So, if it wasn't Mum's doing, it *had* to have been mine.

I think I walked all the way to Martin's mum and dad's in Carnbroe from Whifflet; not a short walk in the middle of the night.

All Mum remembered of that night was that I bit her!

Martin's mum and Dad took me in. John, his father, had driven me to my gran's where I went in and spoke to her. She said, "You and your Mum need to sort it out, I can't help you." I went to Mum's, who didn't want to sort it out. So, Martin's dad came and picked me up, I collected the things I needed for college and we left.

At sixteen I had to apply for homelessness. I couldn't just move in with Martin's mum and dad, nor did I want to. Martin and I had only been together a short while. After six months of staying with them, I was moved into a high rise flat, 21 Dunbeth Court Coatbridge. Not a nice place to live, I have to say. My auntie had lived in the block next to mine for a long time and had no issues or trouble. However, I had junkies and Neds in my building, so there was always pee or someone doing a pee inside the lift while you were in it. People having parties keeping the full block up at night. One time we had someone launching things out of their windows, and they hit Martin's car as well as others with a metal chair and a DVD player. You name it, they had thrown it out the window. It was really a low place in my life. My Mum and I always ended up back on talking terms with each other, because I did in fact love my Mum, I didn't want her out of my life. She was my Mum, no one wants to live in a world without their Mum, irrespective of their mental state. She would visit the flat from time to time.

I remember being at one of my all-time lows in that flat because your living conditions affect your mental health just as much as any other factor. I read this, years after moving out of that flat. It is very true, though. Your living conditions really coincide with your mental health; the links are there if you look and seek to find them! The flats were so horrible, so dank and dingy, I had nothing in the flat, either. Due to the fact I was homeless, I got free things for the flat. I got a good fridge freezer, a single bed, a blue two-seater couch, and a mini-countertop cooker. All you really need to start out. That was all I had, and couldn't add to it as I had no money. Luckily, I had family who were able to get me a few things for free over the years. I ended up with a few really nice things in that flat. I saved all my birthday and Christmas money to wallpaper, paint, and re-floor that flat. It still wasn't much, but it was better than I had. They had put ivory carpets into the flat for me moving in, which were black the moment you looked at them. I was so grateful to get and have anything at all in the beginning of it. I can't stress enough how grateful I was.

This didn't take away from my situation though. My Mum had kicked me out, I was sixteen and on my own. I had my boyfriend, who was amazing, and he was so patient despite me being a bitch to him at times due to my own situation, something he didn't deserve. He was a kind-souled human. I hope one day he knows that I ended our relationships for us both. We needed away from each other. Had we continued, it would have ended in a resentment filled relationship; we were still young and both had an equal chance at happiness. Our relationship had been put through its paces for two people who were so young and had no idea how to deal with any of it. I lost a pregnancy during that relationship too. The circumstances surrounding that weren't great either. It was all too much for Martin and me. As far as I am aware, we are both happy now, and he was happy not long after that relationship ended.

I remember the feeling I had the night Mum kicked me out and I arrived at Martin's house and I told his dad I was *so* sorry. He said to me, "It's ok hen. We can talk in the morning." I was sitting on the couch crying my eyes out to Martin. I felt reassured right at that moment. He knew in his heart I hadn't done anything wrong. He knew because I had been at their house for dinner not long before it. I think Martin had let them in on a few things he had to deal with himself, as Mum would message Martin at times telling him he was scum too.

Martin handled it all so well for a seventeen-year-old boy who hadn't quite had the life I had, having no real experience with such things. I often thought of killing myself during my times in that flat. I could have jumped out the window, would anyone really have noticed? I would wonder to myself. I never really felt a part of the rest of my family, partly because Mum eventually excluded us both from it all, falling out with this one or that one.

I stopped visiting my gran after that too, as I didn't want to put her in a position of choosing me or Mum, or having to deal with Mum if she had known I had visited Gran. I felt it was grief my gran didn't need.

I never went back to stay at Mum's again after that until I had to move in when I was 22, after Martin and I split up. She decided to do the same thing all over. One night I came home from work to a locked door from her. She was drinking again and had put her key in the other side of the door and turned it so I couldn't get in. I am a kitchen manager and had been at work for a lot of hours prepping for Mother's Day, one of the busiest days in the hospitality industry. I was supposed to finish at 8PM and ended up on until about 11.30PM, which I had told Mum I was doing. I did this often, even before I lived with her. It's all part of the job when you work in hospitality, as anyone who does work in the industry will confirm. We had bookings and I wanted as much prep done as possible. Then after that, I came home to a locked door. She didn't answer the phone call from me. She left all the lights on as well, so I would know she was in. I had to go and stay with a friend that night. I remember understanding what a fool I was for thinking I could stay with her at 22. I still hadn't learned yet.

Chapter 14

Gran

We move on a few years. I am still in the flat, Mum and I were in one of our off periods of the many off and on periods we had. Always Mum's choice to be on the off period. However, she had messaged or called me asking if she and Kellz could come up and visit; they had something they wanted to tell me. I said, "Yes, of course." I was super worried about this now. They explained my gran had cancer. She had been fighting it for a short while, she had been receiving treatment, but she wasn't getting better. They thought she would have six months to a year left to live! I accepted this news; they suggested going to see her, and soon, not to leave it too much longer at this point. I kept my cool while they were there.

Oh my, once they left, it felt like my heart broke. Martin had been at work; he was a postman. I called him to tell him my gran was dying; I think he ran around his route that day. He got home in a flash. We spoke for hours about what I should do, and how I should go about this. I decided to go and see my gran, and I would put my words onto a card for her to read and help her understand why I had been away for so long. I bought the card and poured my heart out to her about how I didn't want to make her life harder by seeing her, and Mum perhaps not being understanding about it. She was so happy to see me she shouted with joy, "There is our wee Anneliese!" and cuddled me right away as if I had never been away from her. She read my card and explained it was all ok. Kellz had moved in with my gran at this point as she needed a lot more care and was not willing to allow caregivers to come in and see her bits, only her girls could do that for her. She was mobile and able to get around on her own at this point, but the chemo was taking its toll on her, that's for sure. She was struggling to make it to the bathroom on time, as is the way of chemo. She was getting weaker by the day. I ended up a regular visitor and so did Mum.

Fast forward a month or so. January came around, and Gran was deteriorating faster and faster. She was having to get a hospital bed in now. Kellz was struggling with the pressure of it all so Mum and I were helping her as much as we could. Mum had taken time away from work and I ended up quitting my job. I would get Martin to drop me off in the morning at 7 AM before he started work. Sometimes I would go down in my pyjamas, so she wasn't the only one in her PJs all day. She liked when I did that for her. Between the three of us, we did things that no one should have to endure, but we did it laughing; we were so glad and proud we did it for her. It gave us so many special moments with her during the end of her days that we wouldn't have got had we not taken charge of caring for her.

Cooking for her, cleaning for her, getting her tea, showering her, changing her pads as of and when she needed, applying cream whenever and wherever she needed it, putting her on the commode, getting her fresh PJs, wiping her, laughing with her, and dealing with her mood swings. One night she was in so much pain due to constipation, we put her on the commode to help her. She had been lying down all the time, and the movement of sitting upright would help loosen her bowel. She threw herself off the commode and split her head open on what is called an elephant shoe; this is a booster for couches to make them higher, so they are easier to get up from when you become less mobile. We had to go to hospital with her, as we were all sure she lost consciousness for a few seconds. She warned us not to tell "that doctor" about her bum problems. I held her head together for the doctor while he glued her head back together.

Watching her in pain every day, each day getting worse than the next. At times Kellz, Mum, and I would laugh until we cried, and sometimes cry until we laughed. Each day brought a host of new challenges for us to face. We did our absolute best to take them in our stride. It is so difficult to see someone like that in any context, never mind when you are related to them. She had sores from lying in bed all day, every day. Her hair was gone but growing back in, which we all loved and played with, as her head was like a wee baby chick; it was so soft and fuzzy and she liked to have you rub her head to go to sleep. It was cute, and she was cute too. She was a unique character, a strong character, and to see someone you knew being taken down by an awful disease like cancer is hard to bear at times. You always think it can't or won't happen to you. Well, let me tell you, my friend, it can and it most likely will in some way or another. When it does, do all you can to bring joy to that person going through it. Don't make them have to deal with your pain when they are the one dying; this can be so difficult at times. It is very easy to be too busy worrying about what you are losing to forget about them. By being with them while they are going through all of this, I personally found it so much easier to let her go when she did pass on. To see her pain, and watch it leave her face for that one last time. To watch the relief of it come over them.

She had been getting worse and worse each day, so the district nurse was coming in now and giving her morphine. You can usually tell if a person is in their last days from the medication they are on. Morphine is one; if someone is receiving it regularly, and lots of it, it will almost be time for them to leave us and let their energy go back into the universe. I have been present for a few people taking their last breath and there is such a profound sense of peace around it, you can feel it take over the room. I understand this sort of thing isn't for everyone, and that some would rather remember them as they were and not as they are now. I must tell you though, this is a choice you make in your mind. If you only allow yourself to have those memories, then that is all you will have, but if you *choose* to remember the good and understand that it is precious to get to spend someone's last moments with them, then that is what you will carry with you. Giving them as much comfort as you can as they slip away. It *is* a choice.

We told my gran jokes, explained how her brother Cha would be waiting on her and ready to jump the taxi for her. She would have a party awaiting her arrival when she got there. She and her sister Cathy could fight with one another once again, while her sister Betty played the referee to them. We laughed and made her feel at peace as she took her last breath. When she did die, I laughed from nerves. I didn't mean to, and was obviously horrified that I did. I couldn't help it though! We had been talking about funny things, then she was gone, and I didn't want to cry so a laugh blew out of me.

At the end, they are in so much pain that you wish for them to die, as you know it would be kinder to them if they were dead. When they do leave you, it is a weight lifted for you and for them. You tend to find it a lot easier to deal with the loss of someone when they have suffered around you in such an awful way. Where they go from being the most independent person you knew to becoming some poor soul whose pad you have to change for them, wipe their bum, and put cream on them when they need it.

It is not an easy task; it will take its toll on you. Fortunately for me, I had Kellz and my Mum with me and they had me. Our love and bond are what got us through that each day, every day just getting somehow worse than the last. Had we had to do the whole thing alone, I am not so sure any of us would have made it out with the pride we still had by the end.

Kellz and I talk about it all often! For us, despite all the horror you go through, the full experience was and will forever remain a cherished memory for us both. A time that in true horror we helped a person we love to live the best life she could in the end, in the comfort of her own home. She slipped away in her own living room. Peaceful and content.

Chapter 15

Jacquie

In October of 2018, my wedding was just around the corner and was coming up in the next year. My Mum and Dad came together for this event for the first time in over twenty-odd years. They decided to go out with me for my birthday dinner that year; after my Mum sulked a little while and her and Dad chatted, putting the past behind them both. They laughed and reminisced about so many stories I had never heard about before. They left feeling elated, glad they had finally decided to do this. Mum seemed to float a little after it, able to let go of all the anger after all those years, realising she didn't need to hold on to it. She never stopped saying how she was glad she had done that, how it was so nice to have reminisced with Dad. She needed it; it was good for them to do it that night rather than wait until my wedding day.

My birthday came and went rather quickly and two days later I got a call from Dad's partner Denise to tell me my Dad had a stroke while he was at work. It didn't look good, but we would need to wait and see what the doctors said, he was in the hospital. She would let me know as soon as she heard anything. That week I was thinking to myself that I needed to get to my Dad and see him. Denise let me try and speak to him over the phone a few times, but he barely had the ability to speak; it was all slurred and awful to hear and he got upset. I decided I was going to see him. I needed to see him; the urge was unbelievable, thinking it might be my last chance to do it.

However, paying for a wedding meant we barely had a dime to our names. We looked at different modes of transport and my best friend ended up taking us in his car on a 24-hour round trip, on my one day off that week, to go and visit my Dad. We started our journey at 4am, arrived in Essex at around midday, and we went straight to the hospital to see Dad. I remember thinking and fearing what sort of state he would be in. My grandad had a massive stroke when I was in my teens and he never recovered. He had permanent speech and body damage from it, his right-hand side was completely immobile and sore. No leg or arm function. He only had maybe ten words left in his vocabulary, yes, no, fuck, shit, and I can't remember the others. He was never able to tell us what he wanted or needed. He was being looked after by my gran and caregivers for years and then just the caregivers and my uncle, who still lived with my gran at the time once she became too ill to manage anymore.

The fear of my Dad being that way in his fifties was so maddeningly real to me. I was so scared as I walked into that hospital with some kind of presence around me, people were moving out of my way as I had such a pace. I got into the lift dreading what I was about to face that day. Was my Dad now someone who would need twenty-four-hour care and pads to go to the bathroom because he could not go himself any longer? Was there speech damage? I did not know. As I turned to find what room he was in, I saw him. He got straight up out of the bed and walked towards me! This was my Dad's third stroke, I believe. I was flabbergasted, how could this be? I was so relieved about it. The breath I had been holding, I could finally release. He was looking so good and feeling ok. My Dad has previously had open heart bypass surgery too. He has a history of clots, so I really thought he was going to be in bad shape. Instead, I was able to take him home that day! The same day I went down I was able to drive him home from the hospital. He made teas for us and made us food when we got there. We couldn't stay and wait for Denise to come back from work as we had to get right back on the road; all three of us had work the next day. We drove through the night to get back home in time for work.

Exactly one week later, which was on the 24th of October 2018, my Mum messaged me to tell me that my Auntie Jacquie was in hospital. She wasn't sure exactly what was wrong with her yet as she was at work. My Uncle Tam was going to let her know later on that night but according to her 'partner' John, she hadn't been able to speak for a few days now. The day went on and Matthew and I went out for dinner, during which Mum messaged me asking if she could call me. I explain I am out to dinner but if it is important then, of course, she can call me for anything. She says it's ok, she will message me instead. Her message read:

She is in a bad way. Possibly a stroke. Definitely a chest infection, low blood pressure, and a low heart rate. Found in a terrible condition covered in her own shit and piss, with flies on her. So sad really.

I think it best I explain that my family never once abandoned my Auntie Jacquie. She had her original stroke many years ago. My Auntie Jacquie, as I think I have explained in earlier chapters, was an alcoholic. My family have always blamed her other half John, which is fine and fair. She was a dental nurse before she met him and while she was with him, he seemed to change her for the worse and Shaun, their son, came along a year after I did in 1991. She was eventually fired from her job for coming in still smelling of drink or being drunk. Which is a shame, as she was very good at her job and could have potentially progressed to be something more if she had wanted or just made a great career out of being a dental nurse. Instead, she *chose* a path that took her down a rotten road. It is a real shame as she could have really been someone. She was kind, smart, and a beautiful soul who wandered down the wrong path, and despite being offered so much help over the years by everyone around her, she refused their hand or ended up *choosing* to go back on to him. Sometimes there is no helping a person. They need to *want* to be helped before you can positively make a difference to them; it is important for most of us to learn this quickly. If someone does not want the help you are offering, all you are doing is giving up parts of you in the moment, for nothing. They really need to *want* it and want it badly enough. It is hard to know when to walk away from someone, as we all always want to think we can help, but sometimes we just cannot, and it is not for a lack of trying. You can know all the right things to say and do and that is not always enough. What is going on in that person's head is something we can never know and will never learn either.

She was a troubled soul, that's all we can be absolutely sure of. Mum went on to tell me that my uncle was going to try and get her out of that house this time, where she resided with her son and partner. He was going to get onto the social work this time as she had sores from not being moved from the same position and they were worse than they had ever been. On the 25th I was at work; we were so busy and it just seemed to keep coming and coming at me relentlessly, it never stopped. Thursdays are often a busy day for us but not like this. It was exceptionally busy. The busier it got, I could feel my rage building up inside of me. It had been a highly pressurised few weeks and the stress levels were high. I smashed a bowl across the room. The two staff that were on with me that day never bat an eyelid, as they were well aware of all that had happened to me recently. I am a firm believer in transparency, especially to my staff. They need to know if things are wrong with you, the same way you need to know it of them. It's not fair if it is one-sided; you can't just expect them to trust you if you can't be open with them. They knew what I had been through with my Dad, stressed about my wedding, my Mum and Dad meeting for the first time, as well as the many general pressures of doing my job day in day out. I had asked someone to come in and cover the rest of my shift at that point, as I knew I couldn't be in there feeling that way, it was in no way productive to anyone at all. I managed to get someone to cover the rest of my shift, from 3 PM until 8 PM. I had run this past my pub manager, of course, so he was aware and he was working that day anyway. Chris came in for me and I went into the office and sat on the chair to take my shoes off. I remember sinking into that chair as if someone had set bricks on top of me and suddenly, I was struck out of my weighted feeling by my Mum calling me. I knew she was going to see my Auntie Jacquie in hospital that day so expected an update.

Mum and my Auntie Jacquie were rather close throughout most of their lives. She was a frequent visitor to our house, and a big part of my younger life when she wasn't quite as bad as she got through the years. With Shaun being only a year younger than me, he was a huge part of my life too. We would walk past and pick him and Nicola, my other cousin, up on the way to school; such fond memories (my Auntie Jacquie and Catherine live next door to each other, in different flat buildings). We would pick them up and all walk to school together each morning when we lived on Daldowie St. I remember it like it was yesterday, Paul and Nicola used to steal the heat from my hands when I was three on the way to school. Mum and I would head into Gran's as it was on the way to the school. I was the little radiator, they would say. Mum and Auntie Jacquie were close in part I think because they thought similarly, and felt they knew each other's pain and they confided in each other over that.

Mum called me that day and told me things I never thought I could hear about a person in my life, never mind it being someone I loved. Mum went on to tell me there were signs of severe neglect to Auntie Jacquie, she had what looked like cigarette burns on her skin, bruises on her body that were not from sores, she had cuts on her, maggots in her legs (which explained the flies on and around her), her toenails had curled round and were growing into her skin, and her feet were jet black. It was clear abuse and neglect. While I was on the phone, another manager came into the office to get a cigarette. I politely asked them to leave me, they did, and they must have run up the stairs and immediately alerted Luke, the pub manager, asking, "Do you know what's wrong with Annie?" Luke came through the door what felt like mere seconds later, I was still on the phone to my Mum. Mum was hysterical as I tried to calm her down through my own tears. She calmed down and was obviously and rightly disgusted and outraged. We had been getting slammed at work and I knew every minute of Luke's time was precious as he sat with me, patiently waiting for me to come off the phone. I finally came off the phone and explained how lucky it was I had got my shift covered, as after that information, I don't think I could have coped well if the day's trade had lasted into the night. I was truly speechless after the call; I could not believe what I had just heard come from my Mum. How could you let anyone become so degraded?

I sat for a while, unable to find the words to tell Luke what had actually happened on the phone. I sat there trying to scrape any sense of my vocabulary together to string those words to him, to give him an understanding of what had been said to me, why I was speechless. I could not repeat them, **I could not**; to repeat them was to make them real to me. Admit they were true, but I simply couldn't do it! It wasn't in me to actually say the words and even to this day it upsets me every time I speak the words "she had maggots in her legs!". It is absolutely impossible to even fathom it, never mind knowing it to be a true fact and to someone you love. I found a way to tell him and that was by sending it in a message. I remember saying to him, "I know when I come to you, you know that it's always a stinker of a story," (meaning a great story but drowned in sadness or pain or a craziness most can't imagine) but I said to him, "I know so many things must be running through your head as to what this could be and why, BUT you will not be expecting this at all! It's a real gob smacker."

I sat and wrote out a message, which ended at book-length. I sat watching him as he finally was able to see and understand why I was so upset, and at one point I thought to myself, "Can his eyes get any wider?" The more he read, the more his eyes told the story of the horror he was reading and the more I realised just how bad it all was. How was I supposed to choke this down and accept it? Can I accept this? I certainly didn't want to accept it. Why would anyone want to accept such news?

I was so angry; I remember speaking to Luke in such an angry tone and apologising for it and made it clear it was not aimed at him. I felt in that moment that I could have killed someone, and I wanted to literally kill either John or Shaun for allowing this to happen to a person! I explained to Luke how I could indeed, right now, make my way to the house and start swinging my fists. If I had, I know in that moment, wrapped in those very feelings of pain, hurt, and disgust, I could have been capable of murder. I still hate that feeling from that moment, I'm not sure I have ever in my life felt so angry. Luke was reassuring me that he would have felt the same, in fact, he could feel my anger and was also so angry about it. I wanted to punch the wall and maybe I should have! I didn't. Luke sat with me for a long time when he really should not have. I mean he should have, but they were so busy upstairs that he shouldn't have. He did though, and it was a kindness like no other! It was the right thing to do for me in that moment. I needed someone to listen to my pain and my hurt and he did. I was thankful for it that day.

I went home that day and just sat for a while in silence; no movement at all, just stuck inside my head with my own thoughts. It was a strange weekend. I spoke to anyone who would listen while I was at work, as I just needed anyone to help me gain insight, but there was no insight to be found, only shock and horror from everyone. This was the best I could have hoped for, and at least I knew my feelings of anger were justified. I checked in on Mum as much as I could, because if I was feeling this way, god knows how she was feeling about it. Her anger must too have been tenfold on mine. I wanted to make sure she was ok and not trying to drink herself into oblivion or self-destruct. She wasn't; she was staying strong despite everything that was going on. I asked her to come and stay with me on the Sunday night, as she always came on a Monday anyway. I had asked her to so we could get up early, go out and do something together, cheer her up a bit. She came over and I made her dinner. We chilled and laughed loads on the Sunday, and made a plan for the Monday.

Monday came, we got up early doors. As far as we knew, Auntie Jacquie was now sitting up and talking, people thought she was recovering. Except Mum had told me they couldn't get any fluids into her and they couldn't get a food tube into her either. I explained to Matt then that she was going to die. "The lack of alcohol will kill her as well," I said. We got up, had breakfast, went for showers and we were ready to leave. Mum was getting her final pee in before we left, as was Mum's way.

Her phone rang, and she called to me to answer it for her. I shouted back, "It's Uncle Tam."

She said, "Tell him I am peeing, haha!" I answered it and explained that Mum was indisposed, but she wouldn't be a moment.

He stopped me in my tracks and said, "Anneliese, hen, tell your Mum Jacquie is in a bad way. We have been sent for."

I told him I would get her to the hospital as fast as I could. I hung up and said "Mum! MOVE!" as I told her the situation. Her fight or flight mode kicked in, and she was in fight mode. I made a clear course of action and she was focused and ready to go.

We went and collected money from the bank and called a taxi. It felt like the longest wait of our lives. But finally, the taxi arrived, and we were on our way. Mum was getting that antsy feeling in the taxi; afraid she wouldn't get there before it happened! She was saying to me, "Aww please let me get there in time." The taxi driver had tried to make small talk and it was one of those moments in life I knew he regretted. Mum explained we were going to the hospital because her sister was dying. The taxi drove on and the ants in Mum's pants got worse. We were minutes away from the hospital when Mum got a text (not a call, or simply waiting until we arrived to tell her) that simply read, "She is gone." from my uncle! Mum let out a noise I don't think I had heard her make in a long time, maybe since Paul died. She was distraught to say the least. In the taxi, she was so annoyed about having received that news in a text! I had to calm her down before we got there, and explain that it wasn't worth it, even though we were in agreement. I explained her anger was better defused than directed. We arrived at the hospital, and I am not sure I had ever seen Mum move so fast in all my life. She was off as if it were a race, while I carried all her bags and tried to keep up running behind her. We rushed down the hall and got to the ward where we could see our family.

GRIEF

Mum and I got the chance to see her. I could not believe my eyes when I saw her! I was there with my Auntie Angie. Auntie Jacquie looked awful, truly dreadful. She was so thin you could see all her bones, she was bruised, and there was a smell coming from her, and it was not from her excrement leaving her body. It was a rotten smell, like dead flesh, because there was dead flesh on her. Already rotting while she was still alive. I saw her feet, they were black, jet black and rotting! She was so incredibly thin you could see her full knee bone through the sheet, it was so easy to make out. It was sad as instead of thinking, "That's my auntie lying there" I could not help but inspect her condition. It was really hard to believe that what people had told us, but seeing it was a whole other thing. When we were looking at her it felt so real, it was time to accept it now! It had *really* happened to her.

My family and I were forced to leave the room as John had shown up wanting to see her. He needed a police escort to go in and stand with him due to the circumstances surrounding her death. They were trying to track down Shaun too. He was just as much to blame; he lived with them too as far as everyone knew. The police went to the house to break the door down to no avail, but they were taking possession of the house to carry out their investigation.

So, John got to see her and left. I called Matt to let him know what was going on. I said to Mum and Kellz, "Let's get out of here; there is nothing left here for either of you. I will take us out for dinner, and we can have a few drinks to send her off in the only way that was fitting to do so in her honour."

We went to The Mint in Coatbridge and I got Matthew to meet us there. He arrived a little later, so we ordered for him and asked them to wait for him to come. We had a few drinks in the meantime. We all had such a good laugh and reminisced about Jacquie; the good and the bad, the laugh and the sad. Mum said it was exactly what we needed, and she was so grateful I took them there. I made her understand there was a better way to deal with things than anger, pain and hurt. You can choose to celebrate the person for everything that was good, bad, and ugly. Celebrate the fact you got to know a person, celebrate their flaws, their life, no matter the circumstances surrounding how they lived it. They still lived *their* life. It's a person's right to choose how they live, whether we disagree with that choice or not. Even if we hate them for it! You rule your *own* life, so everyone else has that right too. Celebrate their choices and don't let the sadness and anger take you over.

We raised our glass several times for Auntie Jacquie, as she wouldn't have had it any other way.

We laughed in her honour. Felt the joy she imprinted in our memories. She deserved the best send-off, and we gave her it!

Chapter 16

The Silence

After Jacquie died and her funeral passed, my Dad had decided to rush back to work. He had decided as a wedding gift he would contribute to the wedding, in an attempt to pay for it on his own. He had been making steady payments for a while, but when he had the stroke, I said to him not to worry about any money. I knew he would need to take time off work and he wouldn't have the money to continue his gift idea. He refused and demanded that he would pay me the money. I obviously had a battle with him, but he was determined. He rushed back to work when I explicitly asked him not to and explained he needed to take it easy before causing himself another stroke. He didn't listen. He was only part-time, though, meaning he still wouldn't be able to afford to pay for the wedding. Instead of accepting that, he decided to become extremely distant. What went from being messages every day, fell to once a week, then he finally stopped messaging me two weeks before Christmas of 2018.

I couldn't even tell anyone about it at the time, as my Dad had asked me to keep it a secret between me, him and Matt. Denise found out after he had his stroke. It was awful to not be able to tell anyone that I hadn't heard from my Dad. I did want to try and keep his secret and I was hoping he would talk to me again. But nothing; I did not hear a thing from him. I tried contacting Denise. She pleaded with Dad, trying to help him see sense and speak to me. I just messaged him persistently to no avail. I messaged as much as I could, but as time passed, I lost more and more hope of him coming back into my life. I felt myself getting more and more angry, as no one had done anything wrong, so why had he made this decision? A decision that would exclude him from the wedding. I messaged him to inform him I was going to cancel his kilt hire, as I wasn't paying all that money for someone who wasn't going to be there. He still didn't reply. I told Denise too and she tried to plead with me to keep it, saying that she would try and fix it, but at this point, it was nearly February and months had gone past now. I felt there was no way we were repairing this at all.

While all of this was going on, my work wanted to try and move my location, which for someone with my anxiety, is such a *huge* thing. It caused me so much stress, and after everything that had happened over the last few months, I could no longer cope. I still had my Dad's stroke, and Auntie Jacquie's death on my mind; burned in and trying to process it, then my Dad deciding not to talk to me all while I was trying to pay for and plan my wedding. It was too much, and I ended up off work sick. My Mum forced me to go to the doctor's because I was having a breakdown. I was shaking, panicking, and struggling to breathe the majority of the time. I was off for quite a few weeks with this.

Matt and I had booked our honeymoon on the basis that Dad was paying for the wedding. However, due to him no longer being able to, we had to cancel our original honeymoon and pay for the wedding ourselves. We ended up having to take a loan out to get a honeymoon, which isn't the end of the world, but it was more stress to add on top of what already felt like a *huge* mountain to me.

My Dad never came to my wedding, which for him must have been soul-destroying. I ended up having to tell Mum all about it. I didn't like keeping anything from her unless it was for her own protection. I sat her down as she had asked, "Have you heard from Dad?" for the one-millionth time, and I couldn't lie to her any longer about it. I sat her down and explained the full thing. She was so mad, I could tell, but I calmed her down right away. I think my Dad had a lot of fears about coming to my wedding and dealing with my family, but no one would have allowed themselves to overstep the mark, and he missed out on the opportunity to walk his daughter down the aisle beside Mum. However, Mum got to do this solo and that really was her absolute right; she was the one who raised me in this life. No matter how bad it was or got, she is my life's blood and taught me by hook or by crook how to survive all of it. How to keep standing up when I get knocked down, even if she was responsible for most of the knocking down! She was amazing.

I think she could see I was calm; I had dealt with it, and I wasn't going to allow it to get to me or ruin my wedding experience. She calmed down and learned that there are better ways to deal with things than holding onto them all.

Dad was not a part of my wedding, and I feel sorry for him every day for that. It will be a decision he will regret for the rest of his life. My wedding was truly special for everyone who was there and involved in it too. So, he *did* miss out. He missed out for nothing as well, just for pride. Pride is a horrible thing; his proudest moment should have been standing beside me, but he decided to not accept that he couldn't pay for the wedding anymore and he got to keep his pride, but at what cost? He cut me out of his life for it. Don't let something like this destroy your ability to be happy. If he had simply accepted that he couldn't afford it, we wouldn't have been in the mess we were in. I never even told him we had to cancel the honeymoon, either. So, it was absolutely his decision to not talk to me and I guess that was his right. I now feel though, that he knows he was wrong and that he should have stood by me that day alongside Mum and been as happy as she was!

Chapter 17

The Dreaded Day!

I must be incredibly open here and explain how I have been dreading this day since the moment I started writing this. Writing this chapter and having to read it back several times will mean having to take in and accept everything that has taken place over the last few months. It will help me in the long run, but writing and rewriting it will be heart-wrenching! I hope all of this helps you as a reader in some way to improve your life.

It was 20th of October 2020. A date that will remain in my mind like New York Times Square; well-lit and hard to miss. This is the day my Mum was found. I must go back a few days to help you understand what happened. On Friday, 15th of October, my Mum sent me the last message she as my *Mum* would ever send me, it read;

Anneliese, I always try my best to do the very best at a clean regime. I can go to the toilet at work and there is so much stuff on my hands I can literally make bubbles with that and soap, also takes an age to dry I am being so careful about this. Not for me!! For you and how much you love me, and how I even at my worst, I just think how lucky I am to have such a beautiful soul that loves me, cares for me and has put up with me for 27 yrs. No, not being funny you probably don't remember much of the first three. Cathy Paterson's son was cremated yesterday, I couldn't get her out of my mind. I am a nightmare. Oh, in that light note!! I need a pair of slippers. Tell Dad!! He has been asking, I think. Started your Christmas presents. Just love them because I know you will. Xx.

This was my Mum's last ever true message to me before she hit me with Mary on the Sunday following. On Sunday 18th of October, I messaged her to ask her what time she would be coming over on Monday, as I always did. It started with a simple, "How are you, Mum?" She answered me back and forth. But, it took a turn very quickly, as Mum had messaged her sister to wish her a happy birthday and she had not thanked Mum. This was a big deal to Mum. According to Mum, she thanked "all" of us. Who *all of us* were is beyond me. I tried my best at first to defuse the bomb about to go off in her mind. However, by trying to defuse her, she turned on me; which is common for someone like Mum who had such severe mental issues.

She accused me of always defending my auntie and never being on her side. She almost immediately said she wouldn't be over on Monday, and I asked why not? Was it because I was telling her truths she didn't want to hear at the time? Mum had wanted me to agree with her, but to agree would have been to lie. I too felt a bit attacked out of the blue, as we had been talking just before this about how we both were doing, and how she had been getting her hair done regularly. Then, all of a sudden, as I tried to calm her and explain it was only 11:55 AM, there was still the full day for her to say thanks. She didn't need to do it right away. Maybe she had been distracted by several messages or a phone call or someone had come to her door to drop off a gift. There could have been many reasons she didn't say thanks, and not just to blank my Mum; many reasonable ones too.

You can't sit there reading this and say you have never ever forgotten anything in your whole life, especially to reply to a message from time to time. It happens. But Mum wasn't having it. I tried to defend myself to her, and that made me a nasty bitch, as she was demanding her savings back and wanted to return her phone to me as I paid for it. Which, to be clear, I have never asked her for that phone back. Never once have I demanded it or even held it over her head. I paid for it for her because I could, and she deserved to have accessibility to people even if she couldn't afford it on her own. At the end of the day, she clothed me, so I felt I was returning the favour. She then compared me to John, so I asked her if she had been drinking. She again didn't take that question kindly (I found out later she had been, though, after getting her phone back from the police), how dare I accuse her of that. Except I wasn't accusing her of anything, I was asking. She was so nasty to me. I explained to Mum it wasn't fair for her to be so willing to give me up, it was her go-to answer, I had to just leave her in the past and forget about her. She got worse and worse, and I had to tell her I couldn't talk to her anymore, and I blocked her from messaging me as I was getting super upset about it. I didn't deserve to be treated like that for helping her to try and see reason, to help her rationalise her thought process. My own mental health was weak from her previous mental break down. The fact was, we were back in another lockdown that had been announced while I was down seeing my nephew for my thirtieth birthday. It had all built up and I needed away from it all too at times. She tried to call me twice, but I didn't answer as I knew I would get angry and make things worse. That was the last I would ever hear from my Mum in my life!

GRIEF

I spoke at great length to my Auntie Kellz and Dad about it all. They knew what Mum was like to me; Kellz had helped me with her during this pandemic and with fucking John as well. She understood Mum was hard work. I explained to her that I couldn't take it anymore; during lockdown, I think I dealt with her mental health about thirty-five times going back through messages as my reference. I managed to help her and calm her thirty-four of those thirty-five times! Time thirty-five was too much for me. I bet you must be wondering if I felt bad? Yes, I did then. But now I do not feel bad at all about it! I could have never known Mum was going to do what she was going to do. Of all the times I have dealt with Mum in this way, this was rather mild. A part of me thinks she did it on purpose so I wouldn't be expecting her on the Monday, and so I would be driven away from her. It wasn't news that she wanted to die; I had saved her many times before.

This time she was super smart about it, she didn't draw attention to herself. She posted on Facebook saying she was going off it for a while, for herself. I understand if you are reading this and thinking these are all red flags and you are right, they are; for Mum however, they were not really. She had done way worse things in the past with no intention of killing herself. As I say, of all the times she was attention seeking and all the times she really attempted it, this was the only time in her life she didn't send people the goodbye messages to get help. She didn't want help; she wanted to die in peace! The last message she sent me as my *Mum* was how she really felt, and she knew I loved her. It is amazing how three days can change the world. My Mum actually died on the 18th October 2020, or in the early hours of the 19th.

On Tuesday the 20th, Matthew and I got up nice and early and continued with a jigsaw we had started doing a couple of days prior. We were just chatting, drinking tea, and we had only just finished the jigsaw.

My Auntie Kellz had tried to call me and I missed it because she called me on WhatsApp. I think I had muted my full WhatsApp so work calls and messages couldn't reach me. She messaged me right away, saying call me a.s.a.p. I called her back, after saying to Matt, "Awk, here we go something is wrong!" This was at 2:14 PM.

Kellz explained a woman from Mum's work was at her door as she was two hours late for work. They were aware Mum had mental health issues and due to her always being thirty minutes early for work they sent someone to her house, thinking she had just slept in or had too many drinks the night before. The girl got there and received no answer at Mum's door. She didn't know what to do, so she called Kellz because she had sent a message to m, and it had gone straight into my Facebook spam folder due to her and I not being friends on Facebook. If you use Facebook, you will know there is no way to know you even have a message in there unless you physically go into that folder and look.

Kellz said, "I think I need to call the police, I am worried; do you want me to let you know if you need to come over or not?" She didn't want to make me come all the way to Coatbridge during a lockdown if Mum was just going to be sitting at home, drunk and angry. Straight away I said, "No, I am getting ready now and will get a taxi!" I had a bad feeling. An extremely bad feeling; I knew Mum was dead, I could feel it. I said it to Matt from the taxi on the way there. I rushed to put clothes on, pee, make sure we had money and got in the taxi. It took a while for it to arrive, which was so annoying as we rarely had to wait and I wanted to get there as soon as possible. I was in the taxi on my way when I went into the requests folder on Facebook to apologise to the girl who had called Kellz. She called me and I explained I was on my way, but at that moment, she saw Kellz pulling up in a taxi.

GRIEF

I told her I wasn't far away, maybe ten minutes away. Ten minutes is a long time when you are waiting to hear if your Mum is dead or not. Kellz called me, the police had now arrived. I asked what they were doing and she said they were chapping her windows and had rattled her door several times announcing they were the police. I had already messaged Matt at this point to tell him "My Mum is dead!" He asked me what would make me say that, as if he weren't in the taxi next to me looking as me as we type. I said I had never felt this way about the situation in my life. I had been here so many times before, yet I couldn't shake this feeling of knowing she was gone. Kellz still had hope, I think. She explained on the phone they were away to get the battering ram.

Matt and I had been messaging to avoid the poor taxi driver having to hear all of this. I said to Kellz, "Stay on the phone to me, I want to know as soon as you hear it!"

She told me it bit by bit. I could hear them break her door down. Kellz was guiding them through which room was which from the bottom of Mum's outside steps, as they wouldn't let her near the house because they had to investigate it all properly (as I write this my heart and anxiety are playing me like a fiddle). They found her and asked for the paramedic. Kellz was shouting, "Is she breathing? Is there sign of life? Is Mary ok?" Pleading for them to answer her but the police were unable to say anything until the paramedic had told them the situation, even if it is obvious to everyone that the person is dead; which in Mum's case, it was.

Kellz relayed to me that the paramedic wasn't making any fast movements here, and I said, "She is dead, Kellz."

Kellz said, "We don't know yet."

I exclaimed, "She is gone!"

The police officer came out and Kellz asked, "Is she alive?" I have no idea what he said to her from other noises happening around her, but from her reaction, I knew she was dead. I have never wanted to get to a place and also not go to a place at the same time in my whole life!

Kellz was distraught and I said, "I need to go, Kellz, and tell my Dad!". While I was telling my Dad, Kellz, unbeknown to me, had told Uncle Tam and Jaime Marie. I had already made my Dad aware that I was going to Mum's and we had called the police, and even he had it in his head that it was just another time I'd have to do this. He was so shocked to hear she was gone. Even he, like many others, had no idea what to say to me. I let my friend Darren know as well. Funnily enough, I was messaging him about it, and we had a bit of confusion as my phone changed a word that made it look like I was saying she wasn't dead. I had to retype and fully confirm she was dead.

Matthew asked me, "What do I do in this situation?" as he had never really had to deal with death before. I explained he should call his mum and dad and granny, or ask his mum to spread the word about it. But that either way, he needed to let them know as that was how this worked. He called them to let them know and they were also in shock. As the taxi pulled up, I could see a swarm of police officers outside my Mum's house, and I could see Kellz. I think there were only four police officers at the time, but as my Mum's gate was usually empty, seeing all these police in bright colours felt like the army had been brought in to help out with Mum's death.

Before I stepped out of the car, I gave the taxi driver a massive apology for everything he had to hear, and the fact that the weight of knowing my Mum was dead was now on him. He obviously jumped on it, and said, "No. I am sorry for you". I explained to him that he had nothing to be sorry for, that I came into his taxi, and put my drama on him. He accepted my apology and I got out. I walked up to the police and Kellz; the police looked a little confused as they weren't sure who I was. A few minutes after I got there, Uncle Tam showed up with his wife Christine. Why they came round to the house I will never know. I guess they didn't know what else to do but we were all standing outside waiting to hear from the police on what was going to happen next, and it was freezing. Then Jaime Marie came along too; again, I kept thinking 'why did they come here?'.

Uncle Tam offered to go and tell all the sisters, and I said no. I wanted to think first and process what I genuinely wanted to do. I didn't want anyone unintentionally putting ideas in my head. I needed to think, so I knew the decisions were coming from me and not from anyone else. I knew I wasn't going to be thinking straight and didn't want to make any irrational decisions at this point. I hadn't even seen my Mum yet. I had too much on my mind like, "What the fuck happens now?" as I am sure you can imagine. There was a point where I remember standing there with these faces staring at me, and all I wanted to do was scream to them all at the top of my lungs, "Fuck off!". This in no way was their fault. I just didn't want to be questioned in that moment. I just needed to feel like I was thinking my own thoughts and feeling my own feelings. I didn't want to feel like anyone was in my head, as in moments such as that, it is a very easy space to take hold of. Trying to stop people coming in is hard. I got Uncle Tam to go and tell Mum's sisters, mainly just to get him to leave. I know Mum wouldn't have wanted a crowd outside her door; she had a lot of pride when it came to things such as this. She would have been mortified to know that that many people were outside her door for this reason. All standing around, attracting more attention from her neighbours, which she wouldn't have wanted either.

Uncle Tam went off to tell them and then explained that he would go home after. I was invited to go round and have tea once I was finished up at Mum's, and I took him up on this. While we stood waiting for more information from the police, I decided to go and make a few quick calls and let people know what was happening. I called my friends first, Claudia, Robert, and tried Mhari, but she was at work at the time. Moving on to work colleagues, I called my boss to make him aware of the situation. With lockdown maybe coming to an end in less than two weeks, I knew I wouldn't have it in me to be back at work so fast. It's something I already knew without having to put much thought into it. I would not be ready to go back and deal with day-to-day routine. I called him and he did not pick up, so I sent him a message and explained I needed him to call me as soon as possible.

I then went on to call our boss to alert her to what had happened. I always hate to disturb her, as I know she is immensely busy. Again, I called and she didn't answer, so when I hung up I tried Luke again. I said "Luke, I am so sorry to bother you, especially when we are off, but I am outside my Mum's house right now with the police, as she has killed herself. I wanted to let you know right away, as I obviously don't want anything to do with work tasks at the moment." I added that Matthew would need a bit of time too, and I made him aware that I had let Robert know that he might need to manage the kitchen on his own for a short spell. He also knew that if he really, really needed me, I would be there for him, or at the very least, Matthew would be.

The police had taken the time to explain to us what it was we were waiting for; the detectives, as well as a police photographer needed to come along and check the scene. They needed to take any evidence out of the house before I would be allowed to go in and see Mum. The detectives arrived on the scene first and they went straight in past us to see Mum. They came out and asked for a brief statement of when I had last spoken to her, as well as her history of depression and suicide. I explained this was not the first time this year the police had been called to her address.

They said they knew that, and got me to describe why they had been called the first time. I told them all about John and how I felt he was the main reason we were all standing there on this sad day. I advised that Mum and I had a fight and if they needed any information about it or access to it to let me know.

I explained how I had built Mum up, and in January she was doing so well; before John had his effect on her in a very severe way. She went downhill from there; him, coupled with lockdown, meant Mum was in a terrible place. I expressed my concern about how I thought he had hit Mum but had no evidence, so I knew it meant nothing to them, but I wanted them to understand her mindset. They asked about Paul, when he died and how he died. They asked so many questions. They also explained to me that Mum would need an autopsy due to how she died, just to be truly clear on the way in which it happened. They explained this would probably take weeks now, due to COVID, as everything was backed up. The police would contact me to let me know when my Mum's post-mortem would be so I could proceed from there with funeral plans. They also explained to me that I would need to wait to get Mum's keys released to me, as well as her mobile phone, but that I would be contacted about it.

I cried to the police, not properly, just while I was explaining Mum and I's fight and it made me a little emotional. Then I held it together again, as now wasn't the time for crying; not here with all these people surrounding me. I asked the detectives if I was able to see Mum, and they said of course, but I needed to wait until after the photographer had been and gone and then I would be allowed to go in and see her. Only myself and one other would be allowed to see her. Kellz made it apparent she would like to see Mum, but I wanted to give Matthew the option too. I also explained to Matthew very clearly that he was not to come in because he thought he needed to or on my behalf. This would not be for the faint-hearted, and if he felt deeply that he didn't want to, then he was not to come in that house with me to see her. While we waited for what seemed like ages, I mean it was ages, we had stood outside my Mum's house for nearly three hours that day. The officers then took official statements from Kellz and I, where we went over everything in full detail.

I felt a bit impatient on the inside, although I wasn't showing it. I remember wondering why I was shaking and it was because I was freezing. I hadn't dressed appropriately for standing out in the cold for three hours in October. I hadn't even noticed it due to the thousand things whirling around in my head, as well as feeling like I was about to vomit at any second. We gave our full statements; Jaime Marie went and bought us juice and water from the shops. I made more calls while I waited to get in to see my Mum. Weirdly, her front door was repaired rather quickly that day. The photographer arrived, and he was very quick. I assume because she wasn't murdered, and they knew the cause of her death, they didn't need to be as thorough. After that, I was allowed in to see my Mum. Matthew elected not to come with me, understandably, so Kellz came in with me. At times, I now wish I had gone alone. But at the same time, I am glad I didn't go alone. I asked the police if I could touch her, as I had a feeling I wouldn't be allowed to. They confirmed I was not allowed to touch my Mum. They reassured me it looked like she was just sleeping.

She had passed away in her living room, sitting on the floor with her head resting against her couch. Her head was slid quite far back, making it look unnatural as her mouth was very wide open, but otherwise it did just look like she was sleeping. I remember saying and thinking, "Aw, no Mum!". Seeing her was really one of the saddest moments in my life. The little girl I spoke of came out inside me, and she ran away just like old times. She didn't want to be a part of this, where her Mummy was lying in this state, alone and gone from the earth. I turned to Kellz, who had tears in her eyes, and said, "That's my Mum!" Even writing this to you now is filling me with more emotion than I can begin to put into clear words.

She said sadly and solemnly, "I know."

I cuddled her as we both fell apart into each other's arms, and then I quickly said, "OK, that's enough of that now. Let's go." We left and felt just like we had left a piece of ourselves back in there with my Mum. I knew if I lingered in there any longer, I wouldn't want to leave her there on her own, but the thing to remember is *she* wasn't there! My Mum was gone, and clearly had been for a while! There was no point in staying in that house with her even though every fibre of my being wanted to. I wanted to hug her and scream at her and ask her why? Why wasn't I enough for her to want to stay?

We tried to explain to Matthew and Jaime Marie how peaceful she looked, as she did look so peaceful; we could tell she had passed on very quickly too. There was no pain in her face. She was drunk and must have taken a lot of pills. She had passed out and just never woke again. There was no sign of a struggle from her body trying to fight it. She hadn't even been sick, or from the looks of it, even tried. She was unquestionably at peace, and her face told me that; I could feel that in the room when I stood with her. She had finally done something for herself. I know to some reading this, that statement seems odd, but I watched my Mum for years do everything she could to please everyone else and never thought of herself. This was for her; in a way, I was proud of her. She had taken this moment in her life and used it for herself. Some say suicide is the coward's way out, and I think anyone who thinks that has absolutely no *understanding* and is excessively naïve. My Mum did what she did so she could be free, and that's sometimes all a person can want, sometimes living is too much in itself. For Mum, it seemed that was the way of it.

She fought for a long time to stay here on this earth, tried her hardest at times to feel happy, was even starting to feel happy again before the lockdown and John. But those two things were simply too much for Mum to handle. She hadn't come far enough to be able to battle both at the same time. Kellz and I have expressed so many times now that if she hadn't done it then, with how this pandemic has unfolded, she would have done it by now.

We went straight round to Uncle Tam's. Jaime Marie had the car and offered me a lift, but I said no. I wanted to walk, and it was only five minutes round the corner. I wanted to talk to Matthew about how I was feeling, as I hadn't actually been alone with him since Mum had died. We chatted as we walked about Mum and how she looked and how she really looked, how I felt; I explained what had happened while Kellz and I were in there. In ways, Mum looked terrible, given she had killed herself; I suspect she died on Sunday. When I got her phone back and could see when she last sent a message, it was clear her decision to do this was made on Sunday evening. She also looked awful because she was indeed dead for a few days. Weirdly, there were no bad smells, as she would have defecated herself after she passed away, but there was no smell. Nothing really that you could focus on.

So, I explained all of this to Matthew as we walked round. He politely pointed out that he was hungry, as we had only had breakfast at about 9 AM and it was now 5 PM, so he was probably starving. I said no problem, I will make sure we eat something soon. We got into Uncle Tam's, had tea and a chat about Mum. Kellz and I explained to him that Mum had a mental breakdown back in July, so there was nothing that anyone could have done; she had been receiving medical care for her mental health. In telling him this, we were hoping he wouldn't take it as such a shock, as I am sure he would have been. So was I, in ways. I was not shocked she committed suicide; I had expected it for years. I was shocked that my Mum was gone from this earth, never to be coming back. Even though for years she had me on the edge of a knife waiting for the call to tell me she had killed herself, or me having to go and the police to break her door down. I don't think I ever knew what the feeling of her actually being gone would be like. I never thought past the part of being told or finding out she was dead.

Uncle Tam gave us a lift home that night and I just sat in awe of everything that had gone on that day. I was still trying to work out who I needed to tell before I could post the news on Facebook. Mum had a million friends on Facebook, so making a post was the easiest way to get the information out to everyone. I had to wait on my Mum's best friend to finish her workday before I was able to make any kind of announcement. Telling my Mum's best friend and my auntie that Mum had died was an awful and surreal experience. She was truly not expecting to hear her best friend was now gone. She was expecting to hear that maybe she was in the hospital or something had happened. When I said she was gone, she was so shocked and just kept saying, "No, no, aww, Mary, no."

We were on the phone for a while and I explained I wanted her to know quickly but I couldn't get a hold of her. Her daughter Kirsty had told me she was at work and wouldn't have her phone and that she would be home around 6 PM. I said, "Please get her to call me immediately." She asked if there was anything she could do, but I didn't want to tell her without Auntie Carol knowing first. I came off the phone thinking I hadn't missed anyone who was close to Mum. Turned out I had! But there was nothing I could do about it now, though.

I started writing my post on Facebook to let everyone know at once that my Mum had passed. It read like this:

It is with the heaviest of hearts I have ever had in my entire life that I write this out.

My Mum has unfortunately passed away!

She was an amazing soul, but at times troubled.

She unfortunately felt she didn't belong on this earth any longer and took her own life.

I have only found this out myself today!

I appreciate for some this will be absolutely shocking. I am in shock myself here, and I know people will want to message me and so on. I appreciate any and all support given to me at this time.

It is going to be one of the hardest times of my adult life now!

My Mum was hard work at times, but I love her unconditionally. We rode the highs and the lows together always!

Mum, you were more than you could have ever known to me, and I am so sorry you felt that you couldn't fight on any longer.

No one on this earth knew you like I did, and knew your struggles and horrors. I thought we were fighting them off, but sometimes there is no fighting off demons. Sometimes they get in our heads and bury themselves deeply. Unfortunately, yours must have been tangled so deep that you couldn't fight them any longer.

You will be one of the most missed people on this earth. You were loved by ALL! Literally everyone loved you so so much.

I know that the love you had, I will receive from these people at this harsh time in my life!

You were actually and genuinely one of a kind! Truly there was no other Mary Gallacher!

That post received 400 likes, 450 comments, 40 shares, and I also received genuinely over 200 messages as well as several calls of support and love. I remember saying I was going to do the post and then put my phone down, as I was so tired, but I also felt so awake and alert too. I ended up not being able to put my phone down, as I felt if I didn't start replying to these people now, I would never have the time. That was certainly right of me to think; my time became filled so quickly after that. My cousin Lorraine from my Dad's side of the family called me. I had forgotten to tell my Auntie Christine; she and Mum had remained close over the years despite her and Dad not being together. She was calling to ask if it was true. I apologised to them so much for not calling to tell them, it had just slipped my mind. I suppose it doesn't matter how you find out; she was gone either way. I said to Auntie Christine that I had to travel to Coatbridge the next day anyway as I wanted to see Auntie Carol and Uncle Tam again, as well as her. I was going to see people to help explain what had happened, giving them a bit of insight into what was going on in Mum's mind and help them understand the reasons why. The last thing I wanted was anyone blaming themselves for something only my Mum really had control over.

Chapter 18

The Weight

The weight and gravity of it all started to seep in, sort of, during this next period. I was getting calls from the police about Mum's post-mortem, which they told me was going to be the 6th of November. That seemed like such an age away, as this was currently the 21st of October. I started trying to make things happen and deal with everything I could right away. Let me tell you; I had no clue where to start, or how to go about burying a person, or dealing with their estate. I had no experience in this at all! I felt very alone. In ways, I was glad of that because I wanted to make sure I did everything right by Mum and me, especially by Mum, of course. Even though Mum was depressed, she was extremely open. If you started a conversation with her, she would be so open to it and want to get into the nitty-gritty. She and I spoke of death often; in a family like mine, I have felt a little surrounded by death for much of my life. It started with my gran's sisters dying; Mum and I were close to them. My family were all remarkably close at a time. I feel like I had stepped on a train full of death and I have never managed to step off for any good measure of time. It just keeps coming at me.

I think we will all experience that. However, I feel like that usually starts for most at a much older age. For me, it felt like one after another. Everyone was just dropping like flies. This might have been, in part, to do with me taking on the pain of those around me, as I often do. Due to trauma, I often took on the pain of others and was able to absorb it from them; I am an empath in that sense. Mum and I often engaged in chats about death, our funerals, and what we wanted for our funeral arrangements. She would often make jokes too, jokes with a jag as she would call them. Which means a joke that seems funny, but often has a sense of truth behind it. Mum was insured, but not for a great deal of money; her policy was just enough to pay for her funeral. She would joke to me about throwing a sandwich out the window at "them" as I was driving off to go and grieve in the sun; "them" being her family. In a way, she meant that though. She wanted her funeral to be about her and me! She expressed that to me deeply. She always said it should be upbeat and funny with a lack of sadness surrounding it. That was my goal, my mission. In this one last act, I have to honour this woman who gave me my life's blood, and I did exactly that. I had plenty of time to plan now that we knew her post-mortem wasn't going to be for three weeks, meaning her funeral wasn't going to be for around four weeks. I had time, or so I thought.

I was trying to work out numbers of who can attend a funeral and who should attend the funeral too. These are decisions I will never wish upon anyone in my life. To cut someone from a list to say goodbye to someone they loved was truly hideous. COVID robbed us all of what is normal for a funeral or normal for death. As people, we always want to come together in moments like this, put our differences aside, and hug! At this time, we could not and the repercussions for this I think we will not know for years to come. Whoever the psychology students are that get to write about this and use it as a basis for their thesis are lucky in a way. They will be writing about something no one quite understands and that hasn't been documented before now. I carried on about my days, feeling wired and yet hanging in there. Wired from lack of sleep, yet wired from oversleeping at times. Feeling numb, feeling that little girl inside of me run and hide away from all her pain. It wasn't quite time for her to come out yet and realise her mummy was gone. I would let her know when it was. I needed to get a lot done, and she would only get in the way.

At first, I remember being relieved that Mum's funeral was going to be so far away. I thought to myself, "This is amazing, this will allow me the time I need to process this before the big day comes, and we need to put her in the ground!" I had to wait on her post-mortem being done before I was able to register her death, too, which meant I was able to spend that time not worrying too much about anything at all, other than the fact my Mum was dead. I would be able to focus on the pain, anger, and all the in-between before I had to deal with the big things.

I remember the night I came home, or the night after I came home from Mum being dead. I was in the shower, completely feeling numb. An emptiness had come over me and I was standing in the shower, chatting to Matthew, and said, "You know what's weird? I keep repeating to myself in my mind the same thing."

"What's that?" he asked.

I told him I keep saying over and over in my mind, "My Mum is dead!" Repeatedly, over and over in different dialects at times. too. I think I knew I needed to get familiar with the expressions and by repeating it to myself, I was able to do that. I thought also it would help it sink into my mind. I needed to know, I needed to understand that my Mum was gone, she was not coming back to me! I NEEDED to know this, and I needed to know it fast! The faster, the better. The more I said it out loud, the more comfortable I became with the term.

On the 21st, Mum's keys were also released back to me by the police. That was a strange feeling. I had to go to the police station and pick them up from there. I had never been in a police station at all until this point in my life. I was so scared of people thinking that I was in some way there for a bad reason. I mean, it was a bad reason; a horrible one. I was scared they would think I was a criminal.

When I went in, only a set amount of people were allowed in at a time because of COVID. I entered and read a sign that said ring the bell and wait. So, I rang the bell and I stood there. This was the first time I was going to have to tell anyone out loud properly that my Mum was gone. This lovely woman appeared, and I explained I was there to pick up keys for my Mum's house. I had got a call from the Motherwell office saying they were here and ready to be picked up. She asked Mum's name and address, and I of course gave it over. She came back, needing more information, so she asked a little about why they had the keys. I then had to explain how the police had to break Mum's door down and find her like they did. This was definitely a profound moment for me. It felt so real and so unreal at the same time. Like I was stuck in another dimension here, or I had managed to escape into one for a brief moment as those words were leaving my mouth. I wasn't there as I said them to her. It was very difficult to be able to do. To have to express your trauma in a formal setting with people around who can hear you without being able to fall to pieces. I couldn't let myself start to feel yet, as if I did, when would the feeling stop?

I got a call early the next morning on Thursday the 22nd of October, which woke me up. It was the same lady who had called me the day before. Only she was now telling me the good news that "your Mum's post-mortem has been moved." I was like, "Yes! When is it?" expecting it to still be in a week or two. Nope! It was tomorrow, Friday the 23rd of October. This was a relief and a shock all at once. I had already contacted the funeral directors on that Wednesday, and I had a meeting with them on the Friday at 12 PM. He had explained to me that it would be difficult to arrange much with Mum's post-mortem being so far away. However, we could of course go over the arrangements I would like for the funeral itself, and pick out a few things; coffins, music, and such. At the very least I would be able to give him an idea of what Mum wanted, and he could give me an idea of what to expect.

I had wanted an open coffin for Mum, as with suicide it is really difficult to accept a person is gone until you see them. I wanted as many people as possible who couldn't be at Mum's funeral to be able to see her on the day before; within reason, of course. The funeral director had explained that with post-mortems, it is rather difficult to do an open coffin, and it has to do with the inability to embalm the person. They remove all your organs in post-mortems, your eyes, brain, everything is taken away, and embalming fluid is placed into the veins to preserve the body. However, if they had taken all of that away, it is hard to embalm a person, as well as make them look presentable for the families. I didn't care. I wanted to see her one last time, and explained that I wanted to make the decision as to whether I thought people should see her or not. He was on board with that.

I had to alert him before our meeting that Mum's post-mortem had, in fact, been moved so we should get the planning underway and that he would have the body and be able to process the death certificate ASAP, making it all a lot smoother for them. I was in shock again, but for different kinds of reasons and a different kind of shock, too. I had just got my head around having all this time to deal with and process her death before her funeral, and now I knew her funeral would be next week for sure. I now had to rearrange my thoughts and get back into business mode again. It was time to get the game face on and do what was right by Mum. I didn't let anyone get involved at all in the decision-making because this funeral was about my Mum, Mary Gallacher, and about no other soul. It was to be filled with exactly what *she* wanted and what *she* loved. That's exactly what she got. I should explain that I was Mum's next of kin, and I am the sole keeper of all of her things now that she is gone. The outpour of people trying to help me with money was unbelievable, and at first, I tried to refuse to take it, but I realised very quickly that people were trying to give me money for themselves. They felt that's how they could contribute or show how much they loved my Mum, and they did it in her honour. I used every penny I was given for her funeral, as well as a just giving page being set up on her behalf by someone she used to work with which all went to her funeral too. I had Mum's cash that she had saved up with me to use now, and that also went toward her funeral.

Mum's funeral was profoundly a hit, which seems off and a little mad to say, but it was. On the day of her funeral, I put up a post that read like this:

> *Hello everyone,*
>
> *I just wanted to say a massive thank you in advance to anyone who comes along to support Mum today from outside or at her grave side. I may not get the chance later to thank you in person, so accept my sincere thanks now.*
>
> *I also wanted to say to all those coming along or watching, please smile as much as you can. Mum and I spoke of death often and what we would like at our own funerals when they came around.*
>
> *Today is all about celebrating my Mum's absolute ability to be an amazing human being. It's not about sadness and pain. It's about Mum's 56 years on this earth and the beauty she brought to us by being here.*

She was an exceptionally complex human, but she was a wonderful human who would have given everything to help someone else, so help me celebrate that today because she absolutely deserves the best from us all.

Thank you so much.

My Mum's day was to be about *my* Mum. How she touched you in the best of ways. How she empowered you or impacted you. People really got on board with it. When my Auntie Jacquie died, I wanted to carry her coffin for a lot of reasons, mainly because I loved her, and I was strong and mentally ready to do it. My family said, and I quote, "Not to sound Draconian, Mary, but it's just not done!" You couldn't make a more sexist remark if you tried. Instead, they let a seventeen-year-old boy, my cousin, take on that weight, and we wonder why men in this world are unable to deal with emotion. Now, my cousin was probably sat down and spoken to but I wonder how many men aren't? Yet they are still expected to carry this burden. Ridiculous, if you ask me. I appreciate that was how they were raised; however, times need to change, and from a mental health perspective at that.

I had elected myself for the duty, a duty I had actually taken the time to process in my head and the impact it might have on me. I doubt my seventeen-year-old counterpart did. I am someone who goes to the gym every day, fit enough to take on this challenge, mentally stable, and prepared to take it on. Yet, because I am a woman, I got the door slammed shut in my face. However, this was something I had expressed to my Mum that I would do for her since I was twelve. I said, "Mum, I will carry you when you die, because you carried me through this life, whether that was in good or bad, the absolute least I can do for you is carry you in death."

I have empowered so many people by doing this now, which helped me loads and made me so glad I was able to. Saying it is one thing, and doing it is another thing entirely. Carrying your mother on your shoulder, stepping into the shoes of men for once was very abstract at first. However, I was honestly full of smiles as I carried my Mum out of that funeral home. She deserved all I had, and I gave it to her. With every piece of me there is or was. I carried her to the car and set her down for her last journey. I had the exact people carrying her that she had asked me to; the people she wanted never changed, unusually enough. They were all honoured to do it alongside me. My Mum was a lot of things, but she was my life and soul too. She caused me great pain, but it all led to me who I am now and has given me my ability to help others around me. I have helped myself through life by having this ability to rationalise my own pain; therefore, I am able to deal with it, process it, and overcome it now. Ultimately, she deserved the best send-off I was able to provide her with.

After Mum's funeral was when the hardest parts for me kicked in really. When someone dies, everyone has a feeling of dread or anxiety toward the funeral process; understandably so. It's the parts after that most people (including myself, until now) don't think of. They think we go to the funeral, we put them in the ground or cremate them, and we get to go home and go about our day. No, most people attend the funeral itself, and after that it's done for them. For the few of us who were closest to the person who passed, we must take on so much more than many people realise. It is one of the hardest parts of losing a person, I have recently discovered. The hardships of it most people don't need to understand until they are much older. If you are lucky enough to have both parents or brothers and sisters, you might miss out on this for a long time or altogether. For those of us out in the world like me, it falls on our shoulders.

I had to delete my Mum from the planet earth; I had to take her name out of society! I can honestly tell you this is such a sad feeling, and feelings of despair were really surrounding me at the time. Calling the registry office to register her death was so sad. They make it so easy for you to delete a person from the government, which, when someone has died, is the last thing you want to do; to be on the phone to 25 different places to tell them someone you love is gone. The easier this is, the better. When her death certificates came to my house, there was a slip inside telling me the website to visit to get her deleted from all systems at once. All government bodies, passport office, rent office, benefits agencies, council tax, and so on were aware of her death. The list was long, and it was so easy. Too easy, to delete 56 years of a human being from this earth; I was responsible for taking my Mum away from this planet!

The gravity of that is something I think you can only know in the moment. It is annihilating! Destructive to my mind, body, and soul all at once. The woman who brought me into this world so gracefully raised me in the only manner she knew how, stood by me most of the time, helped me when I needed help, clothed me, bathed me, wiped my bum, got rid of my abuser, loved me, and walked me down the aisle, was now summed up on a sheet of paper able to be deleted in a heartbeat. Of course, I didn't want it to be hard to get rid of my Mum, either; that's the last thing you need. It just felt all too simple for a life that was so complex!

Closing her bank account was a moment of pure dismay. I felt like a robber. The people in the bank were truly kind to me. The woman I dealt with went out of her way to make it an easy, pain-free process. She asked me how I had been coping, how everything was going and made me feel at ease. I needed ID and Mum's account details. I had to wait a while for it to process through their system. I was ok with that and the woman was so apologetic for it. The time had come where I had to go up to the window and collect my Mum's money from her account. The man behind the screen asked me, "How would you like it, cash?"

I remember thinking, "Are you serious? Why would it matter?" It wasn't even my money, to begin with. My Mum had worked for this money. It was hers! I didn't want it. I didn't want to be here having to collect it. He handed me this large amount of cash, and I tried to jam it in my purse, which was tough. After that, I signed a form and that was it; Mum was gone. No bank account, no national insurance, nothing. She was really dead! When I left the bank, Matthew was waiting for me. I explained to him I felt like filth as if I had just stolen the money out of my Mum's purse. We fixed it properly in my purse, and I felt a sense of sadness fall over me as I walked with all this money in my bag!

Again, I was able to email about her phone, gas and electricity, Virgin, her mobile phone, and tv licence. This made my life easier, but made how staggeringly easy it was to end a life, a human life, very apparent! It is similar to the first time someone will say to you, we are all just a number and the realisation hits you; that brain-shattering moment where you physically feel the WOW factor of it all hit you! I am simply a number to someone. It felt like she was as simple as this word document I am writing to you now. If I leave this document, go into file, right-click, and select delete, my whole book becomes nothing; from the click of a simple button. It just seemed too surreal to me. A few clicks and she was officially gone!

Then there was dealing with her house and the many revelations that I have found from doing that. I want to share with everyone and anyone who is willing to listen to me or to read. We knew Mum's house was going to be a major challenge. She was a bit of a hoarder, I already knew that, but what we did not know was how bad her problem had become.

Matthew and I had to go into her house and find documents for her funeral. I didn't think this would be that big a task, as Mum had always kept major documents in safe places and I knew where most of those were in her house. We needed her insurance document, the plot document to open her plot to bury her (we had a family plot already due to burying Paul), we needed gas and electricity bills, bank details, Asda details, etc.

What I was unaware of, which happens when you don't live with a person, was just how bad her hoarding had become, or why? Why was it like that? At first, we thought she had only been keeping letters for the last year. We thought it would be a very quick thing to pop into Mum's house, grab a few documents, and be back out. Boy, was I wrong! She had letters everywhere and none of the important ones were where they should have been. We couldn't find the deed for the plot, which was one of the key ones we needed for our meeting on the Friday. We went through five drawers filled with letters, as well as four to six plastic tubs full of letters dating back to 2002. There was unopened junk mail that she had kept in these tubs and boxes, the extent of Mum's problem was well-hidden. She has always had an issue parting with things in her life. We eventually gave up, took what we could find, and got out as they said I didn't need the deed if I couldn't find it. They would be able to get a copy, so not to worry. We had gone in intending on spending thirty minutes to an hour, we ended up there for three hours give or take a minute or two. Mentally, it was draining for us both because it was only a small glimpse of what was to come. I didn't touch Mum's house until her funeral was out of the way, done and dusted. I didn't think taking on both of these challenges at the same time was a wise idea.

My Auntie Carol helped me the most with the house. I didn't want anyone in my Mum's house, touching her stuff or maybe binning something I might not have wanted them to. It is a deeply personal thing to do. I got to relive my whole life through my Mum's eyes. I had a story to tell for literally every item we found within that house. The scary part was the realisation that, and I say this with great gravity, your house reflects your mind. At least in Mum's case it was, and I can imagine in most cases it must also be true. Mum's house was scary that way; she had held onto things none of us should have held on to over the years. I took photos of anything she had kept, to send to my Dad or my Auntie Carol and Auntie Kellz, so they too could be in shock and awe. I mean, she had kept every single letter since 2002. We were absolutely in for a good time!

We started slow and worked our way through the house, room by room. We started in the living room, the easiest - or so we thought. We found more letters as we went on in so many other random places. Being back in Mum's house itself at times was so odd. There was a real emptiness and eerie feeling about it. I had never been in that house without her there in a long time; we are talking fifteen years now. Even when I was there alone, I knew she would be coming home soon from somewhere and that she was coming back to me. To be in her house knowing she wasn't at any minute about to burst through the front door and rush to the loo for a pee like she always did was a real kick in the mouth. It filled me with such emptiness, and anger too, but mainly emptiness. Numbness too, I guess. Emptiness is a hard feeling to describe if you have never felt it before. It is sort of like being kicked in the stomach, but there is no pain after it. Just that initial feeling that takes your breath away from you. Not an easy feeling once you are in it, stuck with the thought that Mum not long-ago lay dead on the carpet of the living room floor. Moving her things around felt peculiar, a strange sense of solemnness, and voidness came from it. It's not like I hadn't already touched these things, but now it was different than before. I was here to decide what part of another person's life was truly important enough to keep and what, to me, was junk. It was a tough old road.

After her living room, and finding so many old cassette tapes and things Mum had kept since before I was born, we moved onto her bedroom. A real treasure trove; we found her original national insurance number that she had kept since 1980. What exactly was she keeping that for? Seemed all very strange to me. She had all of her eighteenth and twenty-first presents like the plastic keys people used to buy each other back then with all the tags still on them. The one my Dad had bought her was still in there too. She had bedding dating back to before I was born that she refused to throw away. Why? Your guess is as good as mine. She had her divorce papers and letters from all the lawyers at that time. She had my full court case stored away in there, not an easy thing to relive after your Mum has just died. There were bags and bags of birthday cards from mine and Paul's birthdays, dating back to Pauls first birthday in 1986. The number of clothes she had elected to keep but had no intention of wearing again was astounding. I had a story for every piece of it. There were rosary beads, gifts that had never been opened, still sitting. A bracelet my Auntie Carol bought her twenty years ago that she had only worn twice, still in its box, hidden because she was too scared of anything happening to it. VHS tapes with no VHS player to play them on. It quickly became apparent that Mum was so wrapped up in keeping what she already had so well preserved that she forgot to step outside and really LIVE life.

Years ago, my Auntie Carol and I had gone in to make Mum clear out some of the items from her wardrobe. She had a wardrobe with a vanity unit in it. A place to sit and display one's perfumes and makeup. My Mum's perfumes and makeup would probably cause the next outbreak of a virus because they have been sitting for so long, festering and fermenting, some of them had been sitting there since before I was born. Talcum powders, because before moisturiser that's what you got with a perfume. That was a trend back in the 80s and 90s. I know, insane to think of. I honestly think if you had to put any of these onto your skin, they would have burned your skin clean off because they were so old.

We found lots of wonderful, funny, and exciting things in my Mum's house. It was a realisation, though, as we found things a person stored for only painful reasons; her house was the exact same as her mind. Filled from end to end, corner to corner, with trauma. We found every suicide note she had ever written over the years; I cannot begin to explain her need to keep these. They were all dated. I remembered every one of them like it was yesterday. They reaffirmed to me now as an adult, that mine and my Mum's roles to each other got confused along the way. At some point they flipped, and I had to be the parent to my Mother, and these notes really brought home just how much I had to be a parent to her over my thirty years on this earth. How flawless I needed to be, because it was only Mum that was allowed to feel the feelings she felt, and you weren't allowed to feel the same way. Because that meant you would need to stop focussing on her and start thinking about yourself.

She raised one of the most independent young women and hated me for being what she wanted me to be. She wanted me to need her, but I didn't. She raised me to need no one, to be able to put my hand to anything I possibly could. To be a feminist and never need a man to do things for me. If they can do it, then why can't we? She was right. I can put my hand to most things now and do them; if I can't, I will learn how to do it for next time. The deeper we got into Mum's house, the more we found out about her brain and the way she thought. It was surprising to find out that after all these years and her telling me I didn't understand, that everything I had been saying to her was right. In fact, I did understand the way she thought and the way her brain stored information. I also taught her how to change that behaviour, as I did for myself. She was learning; I could see that too. The things I had been teaching her she had been starting to implement before the lockdown hit. It was all just too much for Mum.

When I was young, we were poor. When we moved into our house in Dundyvan Rd, as Mum would say, "We didn't have a pot to piss in." A charity called S.V.D.P., a church organisation that helps people get furniture, electrical appliances, dishes, etc., helped us furnish my bedroom in the new house, as well as a few things for the living room. I decided it was them I would give all Mum's things to. We donated all her food to the food bank, clothes to the charity shops, and S.V.D.P took the rest. It was a mad rush, as when I was sorting through my Mum's house another lockdown announcement had been made and we didn't think we were going to be able to give any of Mum's things away to anyone. I didn't want to have to be holding on to her house for any length of time, as that wouldn't have been healthy.

Fortunately, S.V.D.P. came on the Friday before 5 PM (which was when the lockdown was to begin) and got all of Mum's things. The man told me he was taking Mum's stuff to a family that day! I knew my Mum would have wanted that for her things; she was a giver all her life yet she was always the person in need, too. They seemed like the best fit. I offered my family a chance to tell me anything they knew to be meaningful to them to take. Most said no, and others had meaningful things that I set aside for them to have. That Friday was the last day I spent in my Mum's house clearing out her things. My Auntie Carol had helped me through the process but she had to work that day. Matthew's mum Annemarie was there to help us take things to the charity shops and take the last of the things I wanted to keep. I spent a moment in there, alone with Mum, and I spoke to her while I was there, and I said this:

> Mum, I am so sorry that it came to this, I wish I could have saved you, but I know it's not my fault and you did it for yourself, and I am proud of you for doing what you thought would be best for you for once. Mum, please do not linger in this house; this house has so many bad memories for us both so leave this place and leave it with me right here and now. Mum, come with me on my great adventures around this world, be by my side for it all. Live the life you deserved through me and be at peace with me, around me, and help me travel this world like you wanted me to!

This was hard to say as it was final, but so easy at the same time. I am a person of science. Science tells us that energy can never die. We had a reading at her funeral that I will place here now so that we can share and understand that my Mum is and will never ever be gone. She is now a part of something far bigger than any of us understand.

> You want a physicist to speak at your funeral. You want the physicist to talk to your grieving family about the conservation of energy, so they will understand that your energy has not died. You want the physicist to remind your sobbing mother about the first law of thermodynamics; that no energy gets created in the universe, and none is destroyed. You want your mother to know that all your energy, every vibration, every Btu of heat, every wave of every particle that was her beloved child remains with her in this world. You want the physicist to tell your weeping father that amid energies of the cosmos, you gave as good as you got.
>
> And at one point you'd hope that the physicist would step down from the pulpit and walk to your broken-hearted spouse there in the pew and tell him/her that all the photons that ever bounced off your face, all the

particles whose paths were interrupted by your smile, by the touch of your hair, hundreds of trillions of particles, have raced off like children, their ways forever changed by you. And as your widow rocks in the arms of a loving family, may the physicist let him/her know that all the photons that bounced from you were gathered in the particle detectors that are her/his eyes, that those photons created within her/him constellations of electromagnetically charged neurons whose energy will go on forever.

And the physicist will remind the congregation of how much of all our energy is given off as heat. There may be a few fanning themselves with their programs as he says it. And he will tell them that the warmth that flowed through you in life is still here, still part of all that we are, even as we who mourn continue the heat of our own lives.

And you'll want the physicist to explain to those who loved you that they need not have faith; indeed, they should not have faith. Let them know that they can measure, that scientists have measured precisely the conservation of energy and found it accurate, verifiable and consistent across space and time. You can hope your family will examine the evidence and satisfy themselves that the science is sound and that they'll be comforted to know your energy's still around. According to the law of the conservation of energy, not a bit of you is gone; you're just less orderly.

**- Written by NPR commentator
Aaron Freeman**

It is indeed a fact that my Mum is out there in ways. I just can't see her, but I can definitely feel her around me at times. She is with me when I need her to be. She was strong-willed, and I know that if there is a way for her to be with me, she will have found it and will be making sure she is near me all of the time. She wouldn't have wanted me to wander this earth alone. She will be watching over me with a beautiful smile on her face, making sure I am ok.

GRIEF

I left my Mum's house that day knowing she would have left with me. I put my key in her door for the last time and went off. We headed straight to the rental office, where I needed to hand back her keys. Like I said, I didn't want to have Mum's house any longer than absolutely necessary. I wanted time to be able to relax and see how I actually felt about my Mum dying. There were a lot of feelings I knew would come once I allowed that little girl inside of me to come out of hiding. At the rent office, the woman was so nice to me. I had to make them aware of any objects that had been left in the house, so they knew how to proceed from there and what to expect. I had to fill out a few forms, sign my name, and that was it. Her house was gone! No longer hers. No longer anyone's, really. I was alone while I was doing this. Matthew and his mum were away to get us a hot chocolate from Greggs. As I walked out of the rent office and back into the street, I felt a little lost. People were swooshing past me and I am not sure I even knew they were there; I also had a sense of relief for it all to finally be over. It was finally "me" time now; time to focus on my grief, my mind, and my body. Take a good look into my soul and see what the damage was.

Chapter 19

Grief

Grief is often, in my view, misrepresented. I think people need to realise that grief is a process most of us are going through for something or other all the time. It is not simply associated with death. It is a huge part of life, and the sooner we all come to terms with that, the better able we will all be dealing with life in general. I have grieved in my life for many reasons. I have stated some here in this book as a brief insight into what some of those reasons were. Yes, some of them are death, but some of them most certainly are not. I wanted to write this book so that we can go through my process and experience with grief over the years. I have always said, "Why isn't there a guide?" I realised that it is because there can't really be a manual, as we all feel different things at different times and ways. I feel, though, that this book can at least help you prepare for what will be the hardest times in your life. Giving you a short insight into my thoughts and feelings throughout my life, I think this will better serve the world. That's why I call it the guide to be unguided; it is a guide to feelings you will certainly experience, but it is not a handheld step-by-step process of how you experience it. I cannot dictate how and when your pain will come as we are all different. I cannot live your pain for you; if only I could, I might in fact try. I can, however, hopefully enlighten you through my experience to a better understanding of the feelings that will come and go and the anger you will feel. The denial you will experience, sadness, and depression, the bargaining, and finally accepting what it is we cannot change.

In my personal experience, I think it is best to go in knowing our ultimate goal is to be able to accept what has happened to us in the first place. This is something I simply did not know at a time in my life when I really could have used that advice. That revelation has come from trial and error over the years. My Mum was also a real-life case study for me to be able to see exactly what I did not want to become in my life. We had a fight about that once. I had said something to her in anger about one year before my wedding. She had decided she wasn't going to come to the wedding because "I preferred my Dad" to her, which wasn't true at all. I forewarned Matt already that my Mum would do this at some point because I knew her too well, and I knew her algorithm and her way of thinking. I knew something would come along and make her say she didn't want to come to the wedding. I was right. I tend to have a gift for noting people's algorithms and sussing them out over time. Matthew even warned some of his friends about it. In anger, I explained to her that I had done all I could in my power to ensure I would never be like my Mum or any of my family. I meant this from a mental health point of view. I remember her so vividly and angrily saying, "AW, NICE! HOW FUCKING NICE, ANNELIESE!" Her anger about such a comment was just. However, I bit back at her asking why she would want that for me? Why would she want her daughter to end up with depression and a drinking issue, like every single one of them has. Why?

She should be happy that I somehow found a better way to live my life. An ability to openly address my abuse as well as openly deal with and express my feelings. I have built an ability over the years to break down and rationalise all of my feelings. Mum seemed to think this came to me overnight, when it most certainly did not!

I have worked intensely hard to get to the mental state I am in now. It takes a lot of soul searching and digging into who you really are deep down inside, then you need to rip her or him out of you and take a good god damn look at it. Do you like what you see? Are you good? Kind? Reasonable? Loving? Lovable? You need to rip yourself down and rebuild from the ground up. This all started for me when I decided to go to college and study my NQ in social care. I was told to write a personal reflective essay, so I decided to write one about my abuse. I couldn't think of a better personal reflection other than how far I had come to be sitting down able to write such an essay.

The college rejected the essay, which tore me apart. The experience of writing it though, was what ultimately helped me to realise, rationalise, and accept feelings I didn't know I had about being abused. It also empowered me, and I started to feel like, "You know what, I am here, I am alive, I'm not an alcoholic or a drug addict. I am doing ok. I am trying to better myself," and that's where my journey to healing my inner little girl began, who had been really taken around the town and then shoved into a cupboard and left to rot. I learned how to nurture her, and for her to become a powerhouse of feelings and emotions, and taught her we needed to feel, and she needed to now play a huge role in my life. It was time for her to shine. She got the part; the lead role was hers for the taking. I repaired all that was broken in me from something as simple as writing an essay. Now, writing the essay in itself wasn't enough, but it did help me really understand how astoundingly real what had happened to me was. It was real. I hadn't made it up; it indeed was not a nightmare I was going to wake up from. I was abused.

My Mum had met a woman called Sharon. She was Mum's friend from a support group she had been a part of. Sharon was a breath of fresh air to speak to, and she too had been abused. I met her when I was fourteen years old. I will never forget the day she came bursting into my Mum's living room and said, "Hiya, hen, I'm Sharon. How are you doing?"

I said, "Nice to meet you."

Before I finished speaking, Sharon was already telling me all about her life, which was a sad story; how she was abused, and how it all came to her through the church. I wish she could have understood that not God, Buddha, or any higher power had shown her that. She had revealed it to herself over the years. I will never forget her ability to openly say, "Aye, hen I was abused by my daddy, he did unspeakable things to me!" I was baffled, astounded, and shocked. Where did she get this ability to be so open and honest about her life? Where had that come from? I remember her telling me she could see the weight I was carrying and that one day that weight would be lifted off of my shoulders, and I would wake up knowing I was free from it. I thought she was a little mad at times. I admired her though, her strength and her ability to say, "Fuck it! I will tell my story." It was refreshing for me to see someone not lying about it or feeling the need to hide it away from society. She would say, "Aye, I was abused, so what?" I can't tell you enough how impactful she was for me at that age. I decided at that moment I was going to be like her one day! Here I am writing this book, and if she hadn't given me that motivation and inspiration way back then to face my fears and overcome all I had been taught to hide, then I wouldn't be writing this for you now. She was a superstar, but she unfortunately passed away young in her

40s, I believe. She was much loved by myself and my Mum. She was my wake-up call to be a better version of myself.

Learning to say that out loud was hard for me. I stood in front of a mirror and said, "I was abused!" until I could say it and not feel things I shouldn't. Things like shame and disgust, dirty and horrible thoughts about myself. These are all feelings people who deal with abuse feel all the time. However, you need to stand up to them. Experiencing these feelings is normal, to grow we need to feel them, but don't remain a victim to them forever; which is surprisingly easy to do. From my experience, lots of women have done this. Fear is the main factor, fear of being judged by men as easy, as dirty, as old goods. Fear of women judging them for being a slut or easy or filthy. These are all real feelings, and some men and women do make you feel that way, especially if you don't own your abuse.

What I mean when I say this is, simply say, "I was abused; so, what?" Is it the end of the world? No! Will I live? Yes! Will I overcome and grow? Yes. See every hurdle as a chance to grow and a chance to gain wisdom, and an ability to help others around you do the same. Strength comes from our ability to become a survivor, not in our ability to be a victim. The only person who can make you a victim is you! It is within your grasp to become a survivor. All you need to do is face it all and be proud of your flaws, use your weaknesses as your strengths, as I have done now. Being abused leaves you with so many ugly feelings. It also most definitely leaves you with a grieving process. Had I known then that somehow it would all be over, and I would be able to accept it all, well, maybe something would have been different. I am now glad that I finally realised **I** had the power in my mind to overcome it on my own. You see, most people don't think or understand that they are the ones who have control over their own mind. They let their mind control them through bad habits built from years of seeing wrong things as children and young adults. There is a grieving process that happens while you are being abused, and then one that comes after it is over.

When you are being abused, you lose a sense of yourself in the moment it is happening to you; a numbness. A withdrawal of the soul (for me, a little girl was created), she and I separated ourselves for my own protection. She came out when life was fun and good; I was left with the great part of being abused. This segregation was key to my own survival. I needed to be able to go about my day-to-day life without people knowing what was happening, as I didn't want my Mum to be taken away from me or killed, as Paul had promised. No one could know. See, if I let my inner me come out when it was time to play and be happy that saved the outer me the trouble of having to also fake being normal and feeling normal too. I was normal or at least I appeared normal. That was the goal. I was actually in clear denial of what was happening to me in those moments of my life. If I was in denial, then to *me*, it wasn't happening, I could be a free and happy little me! No need to worry about what anyone would say, or what would happen to my family if it was real. I cried about it at times, not always sure of why I was crying. I would pre-cry before I knew abuse was coming. Obviously, this wasn't an occurrence that happened all the time. I just remember it did happen a few times. It must have been because I knew what was coming. I feared what was to come. Knowing its horrors all too well.

The horrors that come with abuse are ones I am saying are simple to overcome, but I am not saying you will wake up one day free as a bird. There are and will always be things you carry with you. Over the years, you need to learn to love them and embrace them where possible. Welcome them in with open arms. Embrace the things we cannot change. I cannot change the fact I now have anxiety from abuse and childhood trauma; what I have learned to do though, is embrace it. Use it as my defining feature, a feature that saves me from bad people and harm. Anxiety makes me better at my job, from fear of losing it. It has helped me be better in so many ways over the years. Being abused has given me the greatest sense of empathy. I am able to put myself in the shoes of another and truly feel those feelings from someone else's point of view.

This is a skill that I think all humans can and should learn over the years. As I have grown older, I have learned to become a warrior of my flaws. I will not be defined by them; I will be great because of them! This is not an easy thing to do, but do it for you! Do it because if you are a mess, they win! My Mum told me very young, if you let them get to you, they win! We were never to let them win! Easier said than done, I thought to myself. It *is* much easier said than done. It can be done, though. For me to be a wreck now, allowing depression to take hold of me or my anxiety to overrule me and my thoughts would be just like having Paul still here and sneaking into my room in the middle of the night to do what he would do! I absolutely refuse to lie down to such terms and conditions; ones that I realised I wrote! These were my terms and my conditions. I was not about to sign up for a life of entrapment by a single MAN! Mum also taught me we don't need men to live our lives; we are strong independent women! I was not about to do it, especially for the sake of a single unwell human.

One of the things I really want to talk about is learning to forgive in this life. It is tough. We must learn to do it for ourselves. I was told by a doctor when I was thirteen or fourteen that I had depression and he was about to write me a prescription. I didn't want to be that way, so I told him no! I refused his diagnosis. Why, you might be saying to yourself? The moment I accepted his diagnosis was the moment I gave in to it. Please let me be clear; these are my experiences, and I am very strong-willed. Not everyone can or should say no to the doctor. I was not going to allow this human to tell me my mental state. I'd show him! I did too! Years later, I visited that same doctor because I was having trouble with my anxiety as I mentioned earlier in the book. This was during the time when my work wanted to move me around. He said I had come such a long way on my own. He prescribed me an anti-depressant. I still have them in a drawer nearly two years on because I knew I needed to fix it.

In my view, medication to these things is a short-term fix to a long-term problem. They numb pain as if it doesn't need to be dealt with. It does need to be dealt with, sooner rather than later. I believe we all need help at times, I do not deny that. But after watching my Mum on antidepressants for years, I know they are terrible and they didn't help her. She had a lot of problems inside that no medicine could help with. She needed to face these afflictions head-on, but she didn't want to. That was her problem. Facing it was too hard, so she chose to numb all that pain with pills and drink. Not the correct way to go about it.

Please, if this is you, know you are stronger than those pills and that drink in your hand! Please! You are an absolute powerhouse of strength and emotion and don't let any other fucker tell you otherwise! If someone seeks out your flaws, that is because they have envy or jealousy or a need to feel better about themselves; it isn't about you! It is about them and their fears over your progression. Same with offence. If you are easily offended by things that is because you have an inner issue *you* need to deal with. I can still laugh at a joke about anything, including abuse, because abuse doesn't rule me or control me in any way at all! Abuse is my past and happiness is my future.

There is a term floating around just now, I think for those who suffer from depression, anxiety, and for just normal people in general. It puts far too much pressure on them. It is a term that came around from someone famous committing suicide, it is "Be Kind." Now, I am all for kindness and I think we should try our best to be kind most of the time. This is simply an unrealistic expectation for humans in general, never mind those suffering from a mental illness. I think maybe "Be Forgiving," or "Be Understanding" are a much better fit. We can't all be kind in the moment, but we can forgive, and we can be understanding. I took years of shit off my Mum; I didn't love her any less as I knew her struggle. But sometimes in the moment, I would be so unkind to her, simply because I am human and when you are being hit with abuse like hers every other day, it is so hard to just be kind and lie down to it. However, I was always understanding and forgiving towards her! That's what she needed, and what she really valued in the end! I never left her; at times we went a while without speaking. It was always me who approached her in the end. The thing is, to be forgiving is a two-way street. Forgive for them, but especially for you. Forgive so you can let go of it.

I have forgiven Paul. Believe it or not. I have. He deserved forgiveness like anyone else. I have had people tell me they would have killed Paul. That is a sign of no empathy or understanding and an inability to forgive. To me, this says a lot about you and what you need to work on. Ask yourself, why did Paul do it? Was it done to him? He was broken in ways we obviously cannot imagine. I don't wish death on a soul. Never really have. Yes, I believe I said earlier on I wished ill of my Mum, but that's more from her threatening to kill herself and me as a teen wishing at times that she would succeed. One of those times was because she was battering my head in; upon reflection, I knew I didn't want my Mum to die. I wanted her to ultimately get better. I forgave my Mum for all her flaws, over and over again. She deserved to be forgiven.

I think we also need to go over the fact that sometimes we can't save people. I keep seeing everywhere that suicide is preventable; I am a firm believer that it is. I think it needs to be spoken too, that in some cases you can do absolutely everything right by a person and you can't help them. My Mum was beyond help, it would seem. She had me. I was a ray of light and sunshine for her. I was her case study of how to go about it all the right way. How to grow to be better than your past, yet it wasn't enough. She was on the strongest meds, had CPNs, psychiatrists, counselling, the gym, a healthy eating plan, support all around her, yet she was still unable to come out the other side. I fear that was because she simply didn't want to. She was so lost in the pain she didn't want to leave it. That comes wildly from how she was raised. They seem to think that the more that's happened to you the better. What most of them fail to see is pain should never be a competition. They were starved of love and nourishment all their young lives, yet everything has turned into a contest as adults. Even their pain, physical, mental, and otherwise. What all of them fail to see is what I said earlier; strength is in our ability to survive and overcome, not in our ability to be a victim. When my gran was dying, she had cancer and it was terrible at the end. We wanted her to go so she could be at peace. Asking my Mum to stay here a second longer was asking her to live with that same cancer, only we couldn't see it. Mum seemed to be terminal, unfixable by a lot of different experts too. Why should we have been so selfish to ask her to stay with such a painful affliction?

I have had long term relationships since I was sixteen. I met a young man named Martin; he was my first long term relationship. I learned so much about myself from that relationship (unfortunately for him). I learned what I didn't want to be as a partner, and I found it hard to change while I was with him. This was maybe because I wasn't sure how to change with him specifically. He was a habit I couldn't shake until I wasn't with him anymore. I learned how I felt about sex with him too, from an abuse point of view. There was a lot of unfairness toward him because of that. For that, I am truly sorry to him. He also had so many dealings with my Mum too. Poor guy. He is happy now, from what I can tell, and I am so glad about that. He deserved nothing less than happiness, and I was sad to not be able to give him that. I realised that I couldn't give someone happiness if I didn't know how to be happy within myself.

In 2014 I met my husband. We were so close right away; I knew we would be friends long term. My life was at a standstill at that point; I was in a relationship I shouldn't have been in for my mental state. Toxic is the best term for it. My job and life weren't going well at the time either, and on the 10th of December, I tried to take my own life. Matthew saved my life that day. I was supposed to turn up to work at 6 AM, but I didn't. He called and called and called me. I was slipping into a state of unconsciousness; I could feel it. Finally, my head fell on top of the phone, and I felt it. I couldn't see straight as my eyes were jittering in my head. I managed to message him and tell him I had taken pills. He called my flatmate at the time and they got me the ambulance that saved me.

I have never been more grateful for it. Death is not worth it. We will all die in good time; cherish everything you have as death will be here in the blink of an eye. I didn't tell any of my family about this at the time. I told my Mum years later; her response was, "Now you know how it feels." I mean, she had a point. What I realised, though, was I did not want to ever do that again, no matter how bad the feeling. I have had that moment that I think we all have from time to time, where you feel like jumping out of the window. I had it after Mum died. It is easy to think I will end it, but the reality is life is so precious. There is a finite chance that any of us are here, and I don't think we should throw such an opportunity away. It's a great way to look at it; life is our opportunity. The biggest one we might get, so cherish it as much as you can. Help your fellow man out as much as you can; no one deserves less opportunity than anyone else.

Grief can at times be explosive; the raw number of emotions you go through are something else. They are unexpected and harsh in their appearance, sure to catch you off guard too. You can think you are doing ok and boom; you are on your knees to a certain emotion. These are not only bad emotions either. I have found throughout my life that I have experienced the extremes of all my emotions. Laughing uncontrollably, loving uncontrollably, forgiving quicker than I should all the time, feeling an extreme sense of hope. Sometimes feeling the intense need to run. This is one I get a lot when I am grieving (I don't run, just to be clear). I think the running one comes from a feeling of being trapped, and if I run, I am free to be who I am in that moment. Not trying to live up to the expectations of those around me.

You also experience extreme sad emotions too; these are not pleasant. When my Mum died my auntie told me this dude wanted to show up at my Mum's funeral, during a pandemic, when he didn't even know her. I lost my shit. Now my reasoning was just, but my extreme reaction was not. I was in the shower at the time and I was screaming at the top of my lungs about how stupid that would be. I knew there would already be ALOT of people outside Mum's funeral that knew and loved her, and I didn't want some stranger barging into the family when they didn't even know her, taking up space they didn't need to take. There were so many too scared to come and be outside. I saw red, and my god, did grief make the red a scarlet red colour. I remember feeling just so angry I wanted to smash a wall in with my bare fist. I think the pressure of it all was getting to me. People giving you their views on things they knew nothing about, and this sent me right over the edge. Like a giant game of Jenga when you sit that last piece on the top and the rest just can't take the weight any longer. I tipped over and smashed the ground hard that night. I calmed quickly, but the extreme of the emotion was also so tiring. I slept well after it.

You will feel so many things. The day after my Mum died, I found myself crying in a taxi because I saw a mum walking with her adult daughter and her baby. I was that broken, I was jealous of a stranger because she got to simply walk down the street with her mum and I never would again. I cried in Morrison's because they had Easter eggs in the shop, and for the last thirty years Mum bought me and my partner one, and now I knew I wouldn't be getting one this year. I made sure Christmas was amazing for us, and we toasted to my Mum. Mum loved Christmas; for me to ruin it by crying didn't seem right. She was my reason for enjoying it so much, so I didn't want it ruined with sadness or regrets. You can choose to feel things at times; it is in your hands which feeling you choose to embrace.

There are two ways to look at life; there are the negative ways and the positive ways. You can see everything as bad, or you can flip it and see the good in your day. Every single day an array of good and bad things happens to us. Most of the good things we now take for granted because we are used to them, meaning all we are choosing to see is the bad now. There is so much to be grateful for in this life and world every day, from that first breath in the morning, to the roof over your head, that money in your account, that job you have; so many things that if you break them down and look at properly are there for us to focus on. We can focus on what the neighbour next door has, or we can focus on what *we* have right now. There are so many less fortunate than you. If you are someone who looks down on people, please remember your down is some else's up, so try not to look down on others.

GRIEF

We are all trying our best in this life to live, to love, and to be happy. Remember though, happiness is something you have to *choose*. It is created by you, for you. No one can sell it to you, it cannot be saved up, collected, or measured. It is within you and how happy you are is entirely up to you. At a time of deep despair, I chose to feel happy.

I have experienced many deaths now in my short life on earth. I used to choose to miss and feel sadness for that person and for their loss. I have now seen the error in my ways. I shouldn't have been wasting my time, because time is precious. Time spent missing and hurting when I could have chosen to be grateful to have known that person at all, and to have been able to spend any amount of time with them. This started with Stephen. When he died, I was in a better place so I was able to see that I should cherish the time I had with him and not to get stuck in the mourning of it all. I did for a while after he died, asking all the usual questions of death. Why so young? Why now? Why to him? We need to wake up and see that there is no *why*, only the *now*. Live in the now, be free, and cherish everything and every moment in life. There is so much beauty if you only slow down enough to look at it.

Grief can consume you, or it can grow you. You decide which one it is going to be.

You will go through this with everything in life. Losing my best friend in 2020 was exceptionally hard at times. I really did go through a mourning period with that. I asked so many questions, sought opinions, and they all agreed he left me a bit high and dry. Not really a solid explanation as to why, the seemingly ultimate question we all have when we grieve the loss of something. Then it occurred to me; who cares? If someone doesn't want to be a part of your life, don't keep wondering why, all it will do is destroy you. If that's what's right for them, then that's what's right for you. You don't need anyone in your life who quite simply doesn't want to be in your life. I was upset by this for quite a while, my Mum dying and realising that a person who was my best friend couldn't even be there for me in these moments. My Mum committing suicide and not even a question of how I was doing, coping, or feeling. That was enough for me to realise that maybe that was too much for him too. I was maybe too much, and he maybe needed a break from me. Sometimes, we can be too much for others to take. Especially me. I bring a rather large amount of baggage with me, and that's ok. If someone can't handle that, then it is ok. Just as when I've had to take a step away from my Mum, others have had to take a step away from me at times for completely different reasons, but receding nonetheless. This is what I was saying about "Be Understanding." We are all capable of understanding. We aren't always capable of kindness in the moment, and I hope that whatever the reason he decided not to be my friend anymore, he will find some understanding of it at some point from my perspective as well as his own. I hope he considers the price of losing such a friendship and if it was absolutely right by him and me. I hope it was worth it.

Having to go to court to convict Paul came with an enormous amount of grief of its own. It was a horribly uncertain time. I was still in a place of wanting to be in denial, living happily in the denial of it all. I wasn't allowed to sit there and wallow in my denial for long though, with a court case on the horizon. I had to get up and get the work done. Every day, I dreaded the date when it would happen. I wanted the plea to keep changing as much as possible, so I could go about my merry life, free of Paul, but in denial of what had occurred to me. That came crashing down one day when the final court date arrived. We got there and were not sent home for once. One of the clearest times in my life when bargaining had played a huge part. Bargaining with myself about all the what-ifs. Making desperate pleas with God to help me not have to face this; how much better I would be if I wasn't compelled to go through this? Allowing myself a false sense of hope that it would all go away, and the pain I knew was coming didn't need to come just yet or maybe ever. I would have been happy with either, at that present time.

In this instance, I feel I got to skip a stage as the bargaining went straight into acceptance on the day that I entered that courtroom. I had no time for depression to take hold. I had to accept it right there and then. I was telling a bunch of complete strangers I had been abused. I was lying to them too, as I was holding back information that I didn't want to share with them. I had to harshly accept my reality, and I had to do it fast. It was not easy, but I managed it. Sometimes I wonder if those men and woman of the jury see me in the street and recognise me. I don't know a single one of their faces; a moment I have chosen to blur for now, although I remember looking into ALL of their eyes on the day, to see if I felt like they were judging me. I mean, they were, but was it for the right reasons? I wondered if any of them doubted me. I was taken back to that place when I was picked for a jury myself and driven to recall my thoughts and feelings about the whole process. As they didn't know me, they had to make a brief assumption about who I was. Then I thought about the fact I was only ten when all of this happened, and how did that make them feel? But eventually I remembered, who cares? Not me, even if they do recognise me now or have told everyone my story. It doesn't matter to me. Perspective is a great thing. Having empathy can help you greatly in the search for perspective. Use empathy to guide your way. It will help you and those around you.

When my Mum kicked me out of the house, I think this was a time in my life when grief got a good grip on me and the depression stage of it put its claws into me deeply. I didn't realise that at the time, though. I was so reserved, which wasn't my normal self. I was in bed loads, again not the usual me. I felt so tired and exhausted all the time. Scared of what was to become of me. I had amazing friends around me at the time; Marianne, Lizzy, Fergie, Kev, and many more. Helping me; they all helped me with the house and out of that funk once I was in the house and settled for a while. I was down for such a long time when I got into that house. Really in the depths of depression, without being able to see it in myself. I changed that not long after. There are so many ways to make sure you are aware if you are slipping, and if you feel yourself slipping, to do things to counteract that slip. Tell people how you are feeling right away; don't be ashamed of it, just tell someone. I feel like shit. That's all it takes; it will help you so much. Open up about your feelings; you have no need to hold them in. Who are you holding them in for? It certainly isn't doing you any favours. So, let it all out and help yourself right out of that hole. I chose to do that; now I have a much better cycle. I can recognise myself slipping and pull myself right back up out of the hole. I remind myself that it was *me* who created that hole in the first place, so it is me that needs to fill it back in.

One of my greater griefs is not having the parent to nurture me that every child deserves. Having to carry my Mum was a lot of effort and stress, and she took a lot more of my innocence away from me, and I didn't have much left to lose. My Mum showed a lot of narcissistic tendencies. She found ways to make you feel lesser, over nothing. I needed consistency as a child; I have had to grieve the fact I never got that in my life. My Mum left me at times feeling depleted and invalidated from her lack of care about my feelings as I grew up. My Mum always had to say, "Well, what about me?" when it was already about her in the first place. She had a lot of issues and I don't resent her for any of them. It was all an opportunity to grow for myself.

I did miss it and lost out on it, though. I blamed myself for a lot of years for my Mum's lack of care about my feelings when I was so young. I realised I had to stand up and say, "No! This is not my fault!" I wasn't to blame for my Mum's inability to be a consistent parent, even though at times it was hard not to blame myself. I had to make sure I looked after *me*. There were periods in time I took myself away from my Mum, and as I say, it was for *me*. It is extremely draining to be around someone all the time who has no care for your feelings or your thoughts. My opinion didn't matter, my feelings didn't matter, and at times I thought I didn't matter. I learned as I got older that my Mum wasn't ok. I learned to stop blaming myself, realised I was a good person, and moved on from it. I recognised as an adult that my Mum was in serious need of help, so I got her all the help I could. That's all we can do, help where we can.

When my Mum died, I felt I needed time to myself, but I couldn't get it because of the lockdown. I was stuck in the house, not able to get away from any of it. I wanted to literally go and dig an eight-foot hole and stand in it so I could get that silence we require at times like this. It will be hard to analyse how I am doing fully with a lockdown in place. I will need to get back to normality before I will be able to determine whether I am ok or not. It will be rough; I'm not sure I will ever feel ready to get back into work, as that normality will really exaggerate the fact she is gone. Mum messaged me the most, called me the most, so when I am at work and don't get any messages, I think it will be odd for me for a while. I think when there are days I can't cope with the business or I am getting an audit, the pressure will make me crack a little. Until I experience it, though, I will be stuck.

As for right now though, I am making sure my mind and my body are as strong as they both can be through meditation and exercise. I log each day on Instagram. I make sure I am getting up, no matter what, to do my work out and get my steps in. No matter the weather, we get out and get our steps in. We meditate every day, too. I realise there is a stigma about meditation, but most people need to get over themselves and give it a try. It is just deep breathing that brings you a sense of peace, relaxation, and calmness like you have never had. It really does help. Some Asian cultures have been doing it for centuries (possibly millennia), gaining a better sense of chi. That's what we all should be aiming towards. It brings you a much better sense of self and allows you to release tension all over the body that we hold in certain muscles. We are unaware we are even doing this to ourselves. Meditation brings us this amazing feeling of being centred. I have never felt more centred than when I meditate; it helps us realise what in that day we should be grateful for.

When Mum died, I lost the plot over a Christmas tree at work. I have been putting up the Christmas tree for years now. I adore Christmas, and I volunteered to do it back in the day. Usually, the staff who are on the finish the night before would be tasked to do it. They just want to go home, so it was always a half-arsed job. One year we came in to only half a tree having been put together! So, I said enough is enough. Matthew was back at work at this point. I saw an Instagram of a different member of staff doing it, and I felt so cut to the bone by it. I usually take five or six hours through the night (unpaid by choice) because I just love to do it, and the pub looks great after it too.

Then I saw someone else doing it, and no one had thought to tell me. I know my Mum had just died, but it would have been an amazing distraction from everything that was going on around me. I have an alert on my phone and in my calendar for it every year. I had forgotten about it this year, or I would have told them I would have come in to do it myself. When I saw it on Instagram, I felt as if it was aimed at me saying, 'Ha ha we get to do it and you don't'. At first, I wasn't bothered about it, but the more I thought about it, I was so mad! I got over the top angry again. I didn't mean to, but couldn't help it. Same as before; my reason was just, but my volume of anger was not ok. I wasn't in my right mind, clearly. It was a Christmas tree, for god's sake; to me though it was so much more, and I desperately needed the distraction at that time. So, my feelings were like throwing petrol on an open flame. I messaged all of the appropriate people to let them know how I was feeling about it. I only got one person who gave me understanding, true and full understanding for it. I was so grateful for that; the rest were too concerned with ensuring they didn't feel like they had done anything wrong. My feelings or the level of grief I was in didn't matter to them, because I didn't matter enough to them; they were unable to put themselves aside and think about me and my feelings in that moment. However, I know I was overly angry due to grief. It explains my actions but does not excuse them, I suppose.

When my Mum first died, I went into this mode of making everyone else feel ok about it, trying to protect everyone from feeling bad or guilty. I knew none of them could have helped her this time. I could feel it in my core. I would say death is a part of life, and I am not ok now, but I will be; so don't worry, telling people they had nothing to be sorry for. Trying to help them think I was ok. Mother's daughter, I guess, able to fake it until I make it. I knew though, that I didn't want to be stuck in the sadness of her death for too long because she was so funny and loved that it would not be fair to her memory to be sad. Repeatedly telling everyone that Mum leaving us was because *she* needed to, telling them to make sure her memory lived on. Mum would understand we needed to be sad for a time, but she wouldn't want us lingering in the sadness. Telling everyone this was my Mum's right, she got to choose if she lived or died, and as humans, I think we do have that right. No matter how devastating it might have been to us, she had every right to do this. I had a huge sense of relief for her as she was out of her pain; her torture chamber was gone now, and a sense of calm was over her. I made sure people took comfort in my Mum's lack of struggle and sense of relief I saw in her face after she had passed away. Never to let my Mum's spirit leave you, as well as her sense of kindness and giving, carry those on and use them as a tool to help others like she did.

I was thinking I was just giving people what I knew in a time like this they needed to hear. I was closest to Mum, so when I tell you nothing could be done, believe it. I have had people try and tell me that they knew Mum longer than me, they had her more years than me, so they had a greater right to be sad and upset than me. People have told me she was *just* a mum and a friend to me; how could I know what they were going through? These same people claimed to know nothing of her struggles. I have people bringing a million and one of their struggles to me, and I think this is because I show resilience to it all. People assume because you aren't acting like a head case or wanting to jump off a building, then it means you're weird and something must be wrong, and they press you. I raise you this; just because I carry something well doesn't mean it isn't heavy! To tell someone's grieving daughter you knew them longer, so somehow that meant they had a right to know my Mum's private business is despicable. If people wanted to know my Mum better, they should have picked up the phone and been there for her. My Auntie Lynne pointed out to me that these people were putting their own guilt onto me. She was right, but did that make it right, though? No. I didn't think so.

The things you will experience when someone dies are insane; from people asking for my Mum's living room carpet, to people who should really be messaging and contacting you every day not doing so. It is true that your genuine friend's make themselves known. I have had stranger's message me more than people I thought were some of my closer or closest friends. I have had some people who I thought definitely should have sent some kind of message, still say nothing to me even three months down the line. I had people I never expected to message me send kind words. I have had people coming out of the woodwork pretending to care just to get information. I mean, why they want to know I will never understand. Still, please be expecting all of this, it is not easy and when it comes it is so hard to cope with. As you not only lose the person who died, you lose friendships and acquaintances along the way too. People will try and test your patience. They will all take you to your absolute limits. They will try and blame you for their actions. I know this might seem so negative and grim, and I am not meaning it to be that way. I am trying to prepare you for what will actually happen to you during what are your darkest days on this earth.

They are not easy times. You will be tested to your core. It is up to you how you deal with this. I say one and done. You be nice to them the first time, and if they do it again let it rip. Your politeness isn't to be made a mockery of, especially when you have had the courage to give them patience at a time you would rip a person in two if you could. Because you are in so much pain, you wouldn't even notice you had done it. If someone comes back at you after you have shown them the good courtesy of kindness when you really didn't have to, then that's on them. They can lose sleep over it because you are losing enough with stress and worry from everything else going on.

I do find it remarkable that in this day and age people in their 50s think that time trumps quality. My Mum's and my relationship was not perfect, and if you have ever heard the Eminem song *Headlights* then you will have a great understanding of our relationship. It depicts it fully and totally, including when he says, "But you're still beautiful to me because you're my mum!" My Mum was my everything, and I was hers too. Not a god damn living soul had an ability to take that from her and I. The terror and horror we had endured together was what tore us apart, my lack of understanding (when I was young) and hers too (hers never left) that tore us apart. The mixed feelings. I came out of my Mum, was housed inside of her for nine months. Unfortunately, only the naïve could ever possibly fathom that time could hold a candle to such a tangled web that was Mum and I. We were a force to be reckoned with, her and I, through thick and thin we came together, held hands, and fought the good fight! We wanted to fight together. I did say to have understanding, but I hope to never understand why a person could think that. I have no children and no desire to have them, but I know as a child there is nothing like a mother's love. If you think she could have possibly meant more to you or you mean more to her than we did to each other, then you are crazy from where I am sitting.

With 2020 finally at an end and the rest of our lives ahead of us, I realise so many people will need this book and these words behind them. I hope if you are reading this now, you are taking as much as you can away with you, even if you didn't or don't always agree with what I am saying. It's still good; you are building a picture of who *you* are. That's all I wanted. You are starting to look inside to see who is really in there. Throughout the lockdown and the coronavirus, so many of us will have experienced loss; for those of you who haven't, please make sure you know you will also have a grieving process from just the lockdown. This has been one rough ride for all of us; don't forget to check in with yourself. It can be easy to assume we are ok because we haven't *lost* anyone. We have lost a lot of things, though, our freedom for one, as well as jobs, safety, support, cuddles, and our family.

For some people they will have thought this is a dream come true, using the logic of I hate people anyway. We all think we hate people, but there are a few we like, and being kept from them this whole time will have consequences too. In a world that is already lacking in humanity due to social media, we need to be coming together more and more. The division in Britain and America is at its highest level in years. We need to drop it all and remember we are all human beings; we all feel love and hate. We have that in common, and that should be enough. It won't be, but it should be. There are so, so many things going on, you will recognise yourself in this book no matter the type of grief you are enduring. I have often said to those around me, never say you don't understand because that is an outright lie. We all have one massive set of feelings; we have all had every feeling pressed upon. Just because my pain is different from your pain doesn't change the pain itself. What you don't understand is the reason behind the pain. You definitely understand the pain, because pain is universal. We have felt it since the moment we were born, fear being the biggest one we have all felt. Fear works in so many ways. I was scared of the dark because I was abused; some people are just scared of the dark.

I believe earlier I mentioned the gas hob. That's the best way to think of it, I believe. We can all have our hand over a gas flame, so we are all feeling the burn, but some of us have had the valve opened more on us than others. We know the same pain; it's the depth of the pain that differs. So, take that on with you and have an understanding of people's pains. Even if theirs seems lesser than yours.

That is the same fear with different levels of intensity to them. We all know loss too. I had so many people tell me they had no idea how I must be feeling; that simply isn't true! We have all lost something; your phone, purse, a child in the supermarket, your favourite ring, a friend, a boyfriend/girlfriend, lost a grandparent, the list goes on and on. The loss level is higher, but the feeling is the exact same; some are more intense than others. We underestimate ourselves all the time in this way, as we haven't searched ourselves to look for that level of understanding. Never think your experiences are insignificant just because they seem less severe than someone else's. If you read this and thought, "My fucking god, she had been through the mill," you would be right, I have. There are people in far worse positions than me, and that's what grounds me to this earth. Let's help each other out with our pains and our experiences. Understanding is what will save us all. Empathy is the key to the future of humanity. I want you to reach inside, look and see what you can find in your life that directly relates to mine. The feelings, specifically. Feel my pain, because you know the pain, all you have to do is amplify it to have walked in my shoes. My shoes weren't easy to walk in, but I have made it out all the better for it. I want the same for everyone. We can all do this if we _choose_ to! It really is a choice we need to make. Accept that you are responsible for yourself, your mind, and body, and take charge of it all. Take those five minutes and watch a free YouTube breathing video; start with that, and see where it leads you. You will feel so much better for it. Get up and get that body moving, for *you*. Do it because *you* need to do it for *yourself!*

Take a good look around your house and at the things in it. Are you holding on to things that are hurting you? Read them and get them in the bin, you don't need them anymore. They cannot hurt you anymore. If you can, bin the person hurting you, too. Bin toxic relationships. Remember, to be happy in a relationship, you need to be happy within yourself first. Matthew and my vows went like this:

I vow:

To love you

To honour you

To cherish you

To take care of you, no matter the time of day, how sick you may be, or how long it has been since you last had a shower.

*To ensure to reach for **my own goals** and happiness throughout our lives and help push you towards yours so we can both be **truly happy**.*

I also vow to keep updating these vows as we go, because one set of vows can't cover a lifetime of growing and changing with you, travelling the world together and falling more and more in love with you every day, which is what I vow to do for the rest of my life.

This is what we read to each other, simultaneously, because we spoke and spoke about how a marriage can last. We agreed that honesty and reaching for our own goals to be happy would be what would make us both truly happy. If you have no inner happiness, you cannot really sell happiness to someone else. I am not saying a relationship needs to end because one of you isn't happy. One of you may just need time to themselves to go out there and discover who they are or who it is they want to be. I think relationships all too easily come to an end; divorce seems to be the easy out now. I think maybe a little self-exploration is all that is needed. A separation, yes, a divorce maybe not. Don't jump the gun. Our feelings change all the time; we need to ride the wave. I think if someone is dragging you down and they don't want to help themselves and you have done all you can to help, then by all means consider cutting them out of your life. Your happiness is also important too. Just be sure to look at yourself before you blame the other person. It is easy to blame everyone else for our own problems. Check yourself before you check anyone else.

Your living conditions have a lot to do with your inner peace as well. Take a look at your living conditions and keep them neat and tidy; a cluttered house is a cluttered mind, as I have discovered this over the years. The more cluttered my house is, the more I want to binge eat and feel like shit! The tidier it is, the more productive I seem to be. Stop and process all your actions and how you live to really evaluate what you need to do to help yourself out of a dark and dingy place. Start small and work up to bigger things. If you are in your bed all day, wanting to have the blinds shut, considering death all the time, get up! Make the bed and go in the living room. It might not happen right away, but work up to it. A setback might happen, and if it does that's ok. Get up tomorrow and try again; even if you don't make it to your living room, did you try? Good. That's progress. Keep building at it and keep on improving. Never forget to reward every little step along the way. Your past needs to remain in the past, only to be looked back on and not to be a loop you are caught in; a turn off in the road that you keep taking. It's time to drive straight down that road. I hope this will help get you up and out of this poor state of mind you are in, because we all deserve a chance to be happy. Remember to *want* it. Create habits that are in your favour and not ones that work against your best interests.

One of my core reasons for writing this is so that no one has to suffer the way my Mum did. I'd love for it to reach as many people as possible for her sake. No one on this earth deserves to suffer like she did. Holding onto pain like it should be a prisoner to her. It was truly a harrowing experience; it was never pleasant to watch. I want you to be able to walk free of your pain by telling you here in the simplest format I know how, I have made it this far, by realising *I* am in *control* of *me*! Take back that control and fight for your life, fight as hard as you can, get people to fight with you and for you. No one will be better off without you! Not a soul! I often wondered as a teenager if I would have been better off without my Mum. In some ways, yes, I would be, but if it was a percentage, I am 90% worse off without her. That 10% I'd have lived with forever. I needed her more than she knew. I loved her, and she at least knew that! She knew in the end I didn't deserve to be treated the way she was treating me.

My Mum died for me! She died to protect me from her. She was wrong to think that. She was wrong to leave me for that reason, but it still was her right to go, and it was a choice she was allowed to make. I am still proud of her for everything she has done to this day. I will always miss her. Her death will get easier as time goes on; some people will tell you it doesn't get easier, that is simply not true. Control that; that's up to you whether it gets easier or not. Remember, the goal here is to accept and move on. My Mum never accepted and never moved on with anything in her life. She ended her life alone and drunk.

What my Mum never knew or realised is that she was grieving. This whole time and her whole life she was grieving, but she never understood or came to terms with it. By not facing all the tragedies in her life, she was never able to overcome them. My Mum spent the good part of fifty years grieving the loss of her childhood, her innocence, and being starved of love. She was then grieving the loss of my Dad and her marriage; from there, she was grieving the loss of her son, and my innocence as well as his. She was grieving because her expectations as a parent had not been met. No one thinks their child will end up disturbed, abusive, and then dead. She was grieving the loss of her life; the expectations she had for herself and the life she wanted had been taken from her and none of it was her own doing.

No one had helped her identify these griefs as grief. She thought she was mentally disturbed. She was, but she was riddled with grief that she had never dealt with in her fifty-six years because no one showed her the way. I was trying to show her, but I was too late in realising it for her myself. I was too late! I do not want anyone to have to be too late in identifying it for themselves. Please identify your griefs and deal with them properly so you can move on from them. If we don't know we are grieving, we will never be able to understand why we are in pain. Look out for any signs you are grieving, identify them, and deal with them head-on. Don't end up in the state my Mum was in, grieving over things that were not her fault and not within her control. Don't let my Mum's life be in vain; deal with your problems before they swallow you whole.

No one deserves this, so this is my plea for you all to take better care of yourselves and your mental health. Someone loves you so much and doesn't want you to be gone from them! Make the changes I have mentioned, feel all the feelings you need to feel, and move on. I know my grief for my Mum isn't over, I can't rush it either. I am here waiting patiently and openly for the feelings to come when they come. They will come unexpectedly. I did a workout one day, and as I lay down after it, I was in a flood of tears over my Mum. I spoke to Matthew about how sad I felt to not be enough for her, to be ok with her dying, but how it was also ok for me to not be ok with it too. I was entitled to be angry at her, even though at the same time I know it was ok she did it. Mixed feelings come with grief; expect that too.

Live the happiest life you can, because whether you die young like Stephen, commit suicide like my Mum, or live until you are one hundred and five, you will want to spend your time as guilt-free as possible. Time is your most precious ally, so don't waste it fretting about the uncontrollable, spend it controlling what you can. Your mind is definitely one of those

GRIEF

things. You can take ownership of it, and I hope you do. If you bought this and it helped you, please tell everyone you know about it. My aim is to help as many as I can.

Time is precious, someone loves you, you are the one in control!

Reflect, understand, and overcome!

My Journey…so far.

Acknowledgements

This book was in memory of my Mum, Mary Duffin Gallacher 28-4-1964 – 20-10-2020.

It is her who deserves the most thanks of all. She was really and truly, in all sentiments, one of a kind. Had it not been for her, this book may not have been written, and may not have been written as well as I feel it has been. The lessons for all to learn were predominantly taught to me by the very woman you see above. Thanks Mum, for teaching us all how to live in a better way, even though it meant you living in torment to do so. I love you and I will miss you for the rest of my life. It will get easier with time. I still almost message you every day at the moment, and I assume that will fade with time. Your light and spark will live on through me.

To my husband Matt, without whom this whole book would not have been possible. You stood by me and supported me, read this book aloud to me until we got the wording right! Thank you for choosing to be my family now. I adore every breath you take around me. You are my soul mate, my light in the darkest of time and my Number One fan now that Mum has passed. Thank you for remaining true to who you are!

To my Dad, you have always told me you were proud. Although I point out what some will see as flaws in this book, I love you no matter what; you are my Dad, and always will be. You have supported me in all I have put my hands to. You have, like Mum, always looked up to me. Thank you for having my back, Dad.

To my beautiful friend Claudia, I can't begin to thank you enough for being my cheerleader throughout this whole process. Your words of encouragement and empowerment have led me here. I have a book; can you believe it? I hope, as you have explained to me, that this will help people in the process of life. You are a ray of sunshine through a sky full of stormy clouds; thank you for being my ray.

To my Auntie Kellz, for sticking by me even when I haven't deserved it at times. You have always been there and us witches, we stay together! You are my life's blood, and I want to thank you for continuing to support me in what will still be a horrible time for a while. Soul sisters for life!

To my Auntie Carol, for always being there for Mum and me. Through thick and thin, you have been a constant in our lives, and I know how hard that must have been at times. Mum was not easy to handle, and she had a lot of baggage. You stayed with her and by her, no matter what she threw at you, and for that I will be forever grateful. Thank you for all you have done for me in my life too; none of it will ever be forgotten.

To my whole family, thank you for shaping the person I have become. I understand some of this was not easy reading and you may not agree with it all, but it was honest and I am glad we have had all the experiences we have. Without those experiences, I would not be who I am. I am grateful to you all for everything you have done for me. Thank you!

To Matthew's family, thank you for standing by me in times of deep trouble and pain and for giving me an extended family filled with love and kindness. For allowing me to sing at New Year and be a part of your joy and hope in this life. Especially to Granny, whose support after my Mum passed was unbelievable.

If you were mentioned at all in this book, I want to thank you for all you have done for me. Whether it was bad or good, it was an opportunity for me to grow and learn, and most important of all, to forgive. As I said, to forgive and to understand are our two highest powers, so use them and use them well. Thank you to you all for helping me learn how to use them.

I would like to thank Bob and Aby, my editors, for their patience and kindness throughout this process; without their expertise this would not have been possible. I would also like to thank Kozakura, who illustrated the cover and also formatted this book for me. Thank you all for making this dream a reality.

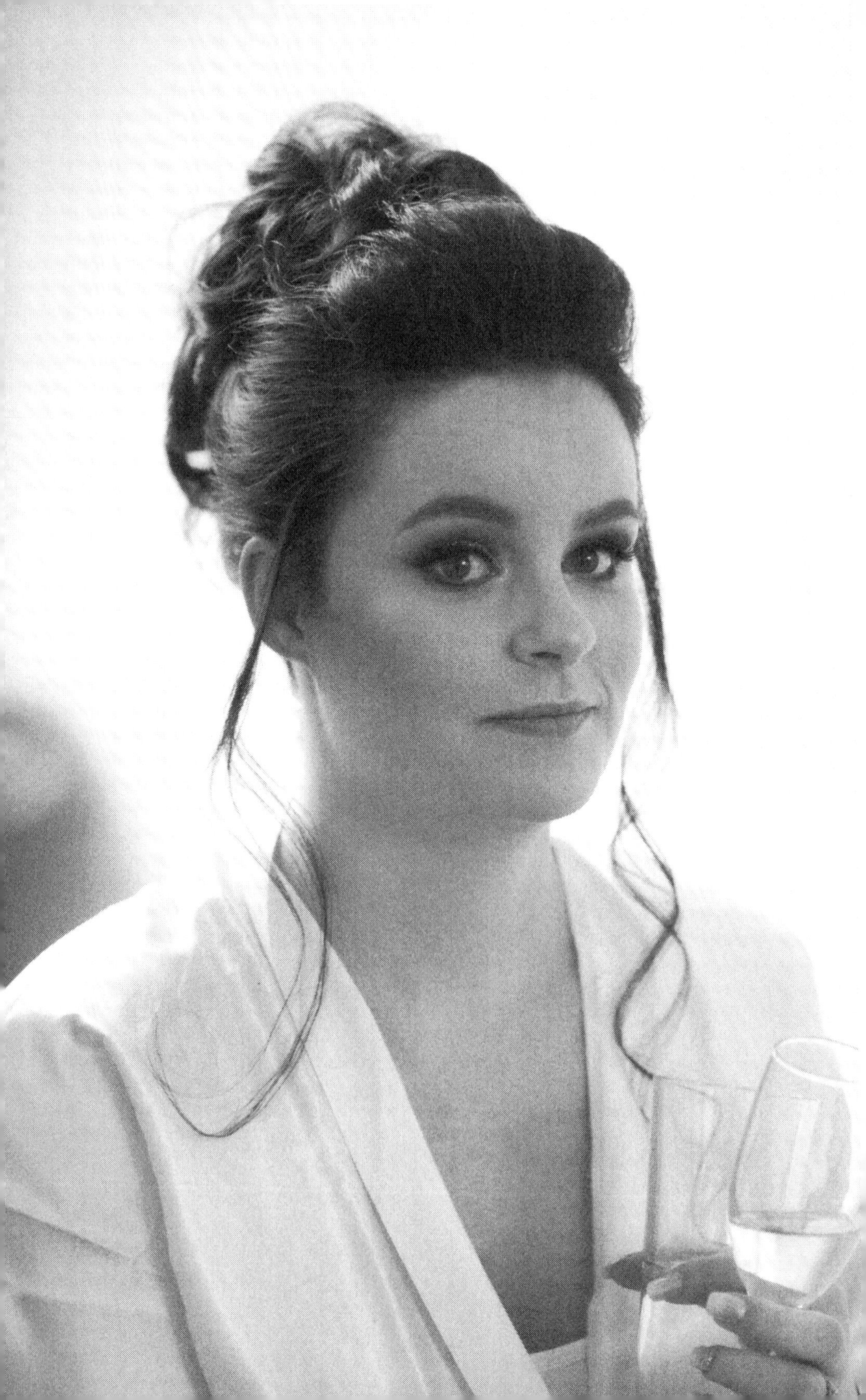

About me

This is me, "Hello!" the photos of myself and my Mum are from my wedding day 16-08-2019. A really special day for the two of us. I used these photos as this was the highlight of my Mum's whole life. She adored it from start to finish.

I am thirty now; I have tattoos, scars both physical and mental, and I adore fitness and meditation. I am capable of writing about this because I have lived it! I am a passionate world traveller and plan to continue in that adventure. I am a passionate empath, and some believe a witch. I have been running kitchens for seven years. I started at the bottom and after three months I was offered to run the kitchen myself, I managed to climb exceedingly high very fast due to my OCD tendencies given to me by the traumas featured in this book.

This was my life and my experiences, a lot of the times we have people with lots of qualifications or a celebrity telling us how to live, I am just your average person floating around life trying to figure it all out. I have been abused and dealt with grief first-hand and overcome them, I want to share that with people.

I have no immediate plans to write another book, but it will be something I will explore in my future.

Facebook: Anneliese McDaid or Grief, The Guide to be Unguided
Instagram: anneliese_fit_ or Grief, The Guide to be Unguided

Printed in Great Britain
by Amazon